CARTOGRAPHY

KATHERINE SCHIFANI

CARTOGRAPHY

Navigating a Year in Iraq

Potomac Books
AN IMPRINT OF THE UNIVERSITY OF NEBRASKA PRESS

Acknowledgments for the use of previously published
material appear on page 183, which constitutes an
extension of the copyright page.

Library of Congress Cataloging-in-Publication Data
Names: Schifani, Katherine, author.
Title: Cartography: navigating a year in Iraq /
Katherine Schifani.
Description: [Lincoln, Nebraska]: Potomac Books, an
imprint of the University of Nebraska Press, [2022] |
Includes bibliographical references.
Identifiers: LCCN 2021046888
ISBN 9781640124509 (paperback)
ISBN 9781640125384 (epub)
ISBN 9781640125391 (pdf)
Subjects: LCSH: Schifani, Katherine—Travel—
Iraq. | United States. Air Force—Biography. | Iraq
War, 2003–2011—Personal narratives, American. |
Special forces (Military science)—Iraq. | Lesbians—
United States—Biography. | United States—Armed
Forces—Iraq. | Iraq—Description and travel. | BISAC:
BIOGRAPHY & AUTOBIOGRAPHY / Military | HISTORY /
Military / Iraq War (2003–2011)
Classification: LCC DS79.766.S36 A3 2022 |
DDC 956.7044/38—dc23/eng/20211027
LC record available at https://lccn.loc.gov/2021046888

Set in Vesper by Mikala R. Kolander.

For Dave Lawrence

Contents

CARTOGRAPHY

1

Power Steering

"I THINK THERE'S SOMETHING WRONG WITH THE POWER steering," Flo says as he drives our gun truck, speeding along a road we shouldn't be on but can't exit.

"Something's wrong with your mom's power steering," Sam says from the turret. She wears a red and white patterned shemagh around her neck, over the microphone on her headset, to keep out the dust. She works with the interrogators but comes on our convoys to man the .50 cal and tell "your mom" jokes from the turret. She's five feet five inches tall, has flowing red hair, and won the base powerlifting contest, by deadlifting 250 pounds, when we were at the air base (beating at least four men), and she can run a sub–six-minute mile. Sometimes she does push-ups with a forty-five-pound plate on her back. She almost never wears a uniform, but on days like today, when she does, you can tell it was not designed for someone like her. It makes her look bulkier than she is, and it makes her hair seem less red, even though green and red are complementary colors.

"I've got some power steering for *your* mom," says Sarkis from the back left seat. He is Lebanese—"one step away from American citizenship"—wears a U.S. Army uniform and a brown special tactics vest, and carries a handheld grenade launcher and his MP-5.

I laugh from the front right seat and wonder if they tell "your mom" jokes in Lebanon. I am happy, at least, that we've shifted to "your mom" jokes instead of the "no-homo" jokes of our training in New Jersey. These started with someone hinting at emotion between two men and immediately declaring "no-homo"—as in "my comment has no homosexual implications"—to avoid confusing people about his intentions. It morphed into people casually attaching "no-homo" to any part of a conversation to reaffirm their heterosexuality among the boys. There were about 150 people in my training class; twelve of us were women.

We missed our turn—or, more accurately, we accidently exited onto another highway—about two miles ago, but there is no way to turn around, and we haven't seen another exit. This is our first convoy since we've been here. In New Jersey, they had a twenty-minute class on the use of the GPS transmitting device mounted in the middle console of these gun trucks. The army trainers told us as air force people we would never see the devices, and if we did, we'd be with someone in the army who would know how to use them. None of our army colleagues here know, or can be bothered to show us, how to use them, so our communications guy taught himself enough to install the device, turn it on, and send messages between our two trucks and our base station. A third of the time they work.

Yesterday, Sam asked me when the convoy brief was supposed to happen. When I told her I didn't know, she informed me I was the convoy commander and that usually I set the time for the briefing. "What time do they normally happen?" I asked her.

"Around seven," she said.

"Yes, then 0700 in front of the trucks," I said.

"Will we do the intel brief then too?"

"Do we normally?"

"Yeah, usually."

"Then yes, we will," I said and set off to find the intel troop, who might know what should be included.

When I arrived at this compound, the guy I was replacing said that things were slow, that the Iraqis were solidly in control of their own system, that the roads were safe, and that we would have so much time we'd be shooting the birds at the trash heap to stay busy. He gave me a notebook with random, outdated information, took me to meet the nine Iraqis I'd be advising, and handed me three hand-drawn maps of the roads we drive most often and the two or three places we most frequently go. Then he went to try to pack a twenty-square-foot rug he'd received as a gift into a four-foot cube to mail to his wife. He gave me a long-barrel revolver with an ivory pistol grip mounted on red velvet and encased in a gold-embossed braided oak frame.

"I haven't figured out how to get this back," he said. "You can mail it to me or keep it or whatever."

Then he handed me the cell phone and said good luck. I received intimate text messages from his wife for the next few days before he reappeared yesterday morning, asked for the cell phone back, and erased all the memory, and he and the rest of his team left the country.

With him gone, the first thing I did was not preparing for the convoy briefing I was giving at 0700, but going through the drawers of my desk and sorting through all the things he left here. In the top drawer: pens, a dried-up yellow highlighter, loose paper clips, the green 5x7 hardbound notebook he used for the first third of his tour and then stopped writing in, scissors, a stapler. In the middle drawer: two empty 5.56 magazines, sixteen loose 9mm rounds, a lighter with a flashlight switch on the side that, when turned on, projected a small glowing rendition of Saddam Hussein's face, a green smoke grenade, two Post-it note pads, a package of mechanical pencils, maps of the road system with known threats highlighted in blue, a stack of blank papers stamped "SECRET." In the bottom drawer: a set of leg shackles, two sets of hand shackles, a key to the shackles, an incendiary grenade, two regular grenades, two magazines of 5.56, one magazine of 5.56 tracer (all thirty rounds), eight loose .50 cal rounds, a container of Wite-Out. I didn't know what to do with most of these things, so I put all the office goods in the top drawer and all the shackles and grenades and bullets in the bottom drawer. I left the middle drawer open for maps and empty secrets.

Our intel troop wears polo shirts that are too small to accommodate her chest and black cargo pants, is in the middle of a divorce, and works nights. She told us about the threats we might have to navigate on the primary and secondary paths of travel. She explained how yesterday a British convoy was hit, on our primary route, with an IED that was attached to an overpass and fired straight down through the turret. Injuries were unknown. She talked about an Iraqi army vehicle hit with an IED, on our secondary route, that separated the rear axle from the rest of the vehicle.

After she left, I conducted the rest of the convoy briefing. I tried to remember the frantic notes I'd taken in New Jersey, despite the army trainers telling me I would never be in charge of a convoy. I had never commanded a convoy before—not even in New Jersey, where they had no mechanism of selecting who got to practice roles we might find ourselves in during the war.

One day, in training, when I was the truck commander in the lead truck, we reported what looked like an IED (simulated, of course) to a lieutenant who had arbitrarily been named convoy commander. We saw raised earth and what looked like wires, so we halted the line of six trucks. Lieutenant Tran—who never left the wire on his deployment to Afghanistan—asked us over the radio why we stopped after our reported findings. "Because we have identified an IED; request EOD this location and alternate route of travel," I said.

"No," he said. "Just keep driving. You're holding up the line."

I repeated our report.

From his position in the second-to-last truck, he said, "Either you drive, or we let truck two pass you."

We drove. Directly over the line of raised dirt and wires. When the ground-burst simulator went off underneath our truck, the gunner jumped down from the turret and curled up across the back two seats. My driver, Ben, a staff sergeant on his third deployment to Afghanistan, stopped the truck. The army trainers told us our truck was disabled and we were all (simulated) dead except Terry, the guy in the back right seat, and Ben walked over to Tran's truck.

"Fuck you. Fuck you, Tran. What the fuck? You fucking think the lumps of dirt with wires are just a fucking speed bump? You fucking think it's okay to make other people drive over fucking bombs? You're a fucking moron. A fucking moron. I have no fucking clue how you are an officer. Have you ever fucking been in charge of anyone? Do you have a fucking brain? Or a conscience?"

Tran had, in fact, never been in charge of anyone before, not really. He sat in the front seat of his truck listening to Ben for a bit and then closed the small sliding window. Ben picked up a rock and threw it at the bulletproof glass. Then he walked back to our (simulated) disabled vehicle to pretend he was dead. He opened the door, got in, and, before he leaned back in the seat and closed his eyes, looked at me over the communication equipment between us and said, "And fuck you too. All you fucking officers. Let me tell you a secret, ma'am: Next time you're driving and there's a bomb in front of you, don't fucking make your truck drive over it and kill everyone."

"I'm not dead," Terry said.

"Fucking great," Ben said. "Then you can write letters to all of our wives explaining how we were killed by some twenty-three-year-old moron officer."

"She doesn't have a wife," Terry said, pointing to me.

"Fucking shut it," Ben said.

Terry looked at me and said, "No-homo."

"Terry! Fuck!" Ben yelled from the front seat.

Terry was right, mostly. I didn't have a wife because same-sex marriage wasn't legal in the United States, Don't Ask Don't Tell had kept servicemen and women lying about their personal lives for almost two decades, and my girlfriend, Annie, seemed too anxious for us to make it through this deployment.

I wrote in my notebook: *Make sure to brief as part of the situation that if we see an IED, we will not drive over it.*

In the briefing, I continued down the list: mission, sectors of fire (which, in a two-truck convoy, is simply forward and backward, not intersecting). We reviewed what to do if we took small arms fire, if we saw an IED (not drive over it), and what we would do if for some reason we didn't see it and did drive over it.

Normally, a trip ticket has detailed info about the trucks' identifying information, license plates, and registration numbers. But we have only two trucks, they are painted to match the Iraqi Special Operations Forces, and they don't have any of the normal identifying info. So we distinguish them by the guns we can mount and the number of zombies stenciled on the side panels.

Finally, I went back over the route, which would take us through a residential area, along a highway through three checkpoints, back through a residential area, and finally to our destination, roughly ninety minutes away. We had developed terms for the status of our movement, which we went over again with our base station, and then we mounted and drove to the gun pit to test fire.

WHEN WE PULLED UP TO THE FIRST CHECKPOINT, THE IRAQI army soldier handed us a clipboard. I was supposed to fill out our trip information for them. Under vehicles, I listed two. For passengers, I listed seven. For the call sign of our mission, I listed "your mom." Sarkis handed the clipboard back to the Iraqi soldier, who looked at it, handed it back, and demanded our real call sign. Apparently, they tell "your mom" jokes in English in Iraq. I erased "your mom" and put down "Lord Byron," which seemed to satisfy the IA. When we pulled away, Sarkis told us over the radio what the IA said the first time he read our call sign, and we all laughed so hard Flo forgot to merge left, drove over a pile of trash (before we could think about not driving over bombs), and accidently exited to a road not on our trip ticket. Schwab, from the second truck, came over the radio with, "What the fuck? Over."

Now that it is clear we are on the wrong road, a road that none of us has ever been on, I get out the maps to see what the new situation is. We are headed north, toward a bridge we know we should not cross. We know this because the map—which, like all our maps, has relabeled all the street names and features to something in English that doesn't correspond to their actual names—has a red X over the "Red Bridge of Courage" and the death count from a previous incident (3 KIA, 8 EKIA, IED-4 ea. 105mm daisy chain, small arms). "Thunder 1"—the call sign we gave our truck—"this is Thunder 2, you are dragging something under the truck. Over," Schwab says.

"Your mom's dragging something under her truck," Sam says from the turret.

We take the next exit and go through another checkpoint, this one manned by a Ministry of Interior soldier. He motions for Sam to point the .50 cal up and to the right as he stands to the left of our truck and hands Sarkis the clipboard. Sam keeps the .50 pointed straight at him. The MOI soldier yells something at Sarkis and points to Sam, whose long red hair is braided down her back so her helmet fits without obstruction. "He says to point the gun up and right," Sarkis says on the radio.

"I know," Sam says.

Sarkis hands me the clipboard. This time we are Ernest Hemingway and our destination is Key West. Sarkis and the MOI soldier are still yelling back and forth, and Sarkis positions the MP-5 more prominently while the MOI brings his AK-47 closer to his chest. I hand the clipboard back and Sarkis gives it to the MOI soldier.

"Stay on him, Montana," Sam says to Thunder 2's gunner, and she watches as we pull forward past razor wire. Montana points the 240 at him as he motions to point it up and right. As the truck pulls away, I watch in the side mirror as the MOI brings his AK-47 to the high ready, nestled in his shoulder, finger on the trigger. Montana holds the 240 on him and settles in behind the turret's shield until the MOI lowers his gun and turns to the other people at the checkpoint.

"I'm pretty sure we rolled him up about two months ago," Sam says to both trucks as we merge onto the highway, headed away from the Red Bridge of Courage toward the right highway.

This would have been a natural place for another "your mom" joke. Sarkis and Flo tell me later that their goal was thirty-five for the round trip, "but they have to be natural." Instead, Flo says, "No shit, somethin's wrong with the power steering."

The trash we've been dragging jostles loose as we merge onto the main highway, driving over a small black and yellow curb divider. "Flo, are you drunk?" Schwab asks from Thunder 2.

"Fuck you," Flo says. "Sir."

"Your mom *was* drunk," says Sarkis.

"She'd have to be to handle you," Sam says from the turret.

"Mayor this is Thunder, Charlie 3, this time," I say to our base station over the satellite radio, which later, after five months of driving, we learn never transmitted.

Flo uses both hands in an exaggerated motion to make the turn off the highway and through the residential neighborhood. We are now forty minutes late for our meeting, but we will likely still arrive before the Iraqis. We pull into a building complex and park our trucks. As we suspected, we are the only ones here, except for the Iraqi we came to meet, who lives here with his detachment of Iraqi special forces soldiers and Jim, another logistics adviser, who has apparently taken naturally to Baghdad. We take off our armor, transfer our pistols off our vests to our hip holsters, and walk inside for lunch while Sam and Montana take out books and stay with the trucks and the weapons.

In the dining hall I notice two things. First, everyone stares at me with unrelenting eyes. Second, no one is working but the guys handing out food and making chai; everyone else that works at this outpost is lounging in the dining hall, watching reruns of FC Barcelona soccer games and sending messages on their phones. In fact, since I've been in this country the only hard workers I've seen are the people who paint the curbs yellow and black and the ones who prepare food. As we sit down for lunch, we receive word none of the other Iraqis we came to meet will be here today, so the meeting will happen later, *insha'allah*. With that in mind, we eat rice, some kind of lentil soup, and *samoon*—freshly baked football-shaped bread that is like the Iraqi love child of a pita and a sopapilla—with the general who would have chaired the meeting and Jim, who has been in Iraq doing work like this for sixteen years and now shares the Iraqis' work ethic.

We discuss with Jim a new strategy for helping our Iraqis develop a long-term sustainment infrastructure. Jim smiles, tells me about his previous job in Dubai, explains the stacks of money he has, shows me a new (simulated) Rolex he has purchased, and eats another piece of *samoon*, chewing with his mouth open. We mention again our strategy and, in the middle of my discussion of cooperative support agreements, Jim turns his back to me and asks the general, "What happened to the fish they used to serve here?"

Frank, Jim's interpreter, turns to the general. Frank is American but was in Iraq, visiting family, when the first bombs fell and, after a few phone calls to the Pentagon, stayed on for the invasion. He relays Jim's question to the general, waits for a response, and says, "The fish on Monday?"

"Yes," says Jim. "There used to be this delicious fish here. What happened?"

Sarkis leans in and says to me, "That fish was terrible, like frozen fish sticks."

"The soldiers got tired of fish," the general says.

"And since they are a democracy now," Frank interprets, "they voted fish out of Monday," and the general grabs his stomach and laughs and laughs as small amounts of rice and lentils spray from his mouth. Some catch in his mustache; some land on Jim and Frank.

After lunch, Frank gives a tour of the rest of the palace here. It was the home of Saddam's famous bunker. The building's facade leans away from the structure at what looks like a thirty-degree angle. It seems to be held in place with a few pieces of blue internet cable. Frank takes us up a marble staircase inside the bunker. There's some damage, he says, from the looters after the U.S. invasion. Otherwise, the elaborate stone statues, intricate ceiling decorations, and marble floors look untouched. We go up another floor and cross the grand space into another wing.

"Here," Frank says, "is where two two-thousand-pound U.S. bombs fell through the roof." The domed roof has two holes in it but seems otherwise intact. The floor is upset in front of us, the marble cracked in places, missing elsewhere. Among the rubble is a U.S. newspaper with a headline reading, "The Magic Touch." We get closer to the hole in the floor and look down at what two bunker-busting bombs can do.

Frank takes us down another grand staircase, this one without a railing, and down another, a dimly lit staircase that smells like mold and takes us into the bunkers. The bunker system, he explains, was set up so that the bunker was composed of individual concrete blocks that floated on water channels. The bunker could house enough people to run a regime for a month, and if bombed, the separate blocks and water were supposed to dissipate the concussive effects of a bomb. The bunker has a false roof, designed to defeat the timing mechanism of a bunker buster. Mold on the walls suggests the water splashed up fairly high at one point, perhaps in the springtime eight years ago when the two holes were punched through the decorative dome, but inside the blocks, nothing looks displaced.

"I've heard," Frank says as we walk back up the dimly lit staircase, "that we missed Saddam being here by two hours when the bombs fell."

"Not sure it would have mattered," Jim says and belly laughs.

We finish the tour, say goodbye to Jim, who wants us to come look at the new Mercedes he bought or acquired or received as a gift. We decline, send Montana and Sam in to get their to-go lunches, and begin to mount up for the return trip. Flo turns on our truck. Before we switch on the jammers, I use my cell phone to call our base and let them know we're on our way back. Tonya, manning the comm. equipment back there, informs me that she didn't hear us call any checkpoints, and she didn't receive any messages from us—but she did get one from someone else, who was testing their equipment in Balad, a ninety-minute drive north of here on another bad road.

"The truck's leaking bad," says Flo as we do the inspection. He wiggles underneath and pulls out a cardboard box still lodged in the undercarriage. He gets us back on the road, and we call in our first checkpoint—to no one—on the radio that doesn't transmit. We pull up to the first IA checkpoint, and the IA guard wants us to move left and stop. Flo tries to maneuver our gun truck left. He unbuckles his seatbelt so he can half stand in the front seat to gain better leverage on the steering wheel. While doing this, he cannot reach the brakes, so we turn but don't stop, running over some razor wire and two cones and nearly running over the IA soldier, who throws the clipboard at our truck after he dives to the side. Flo guns it and we blow right through the checkpoint without stopping.

"What was that?" I ask him.

"Fuck," he says and speeds down the highway.

"Thunder 1, Thunder 2, WTF? Over," Schwab says through the radio as I watch them try to stay with us in the side mirror.

"Sir," Flo answers, "fuck you."

What we didn't see about our primary route of travel when we left it by mistake, and what wasn't part of the convoy briefing, is the road construction that forces us off the main road and onto what looks like a frontage road. Flo again has to stand up to try to turn the truck, right this time, smashing his hands into the radio console and activating the windshield wipers. He has enough speed to get us off the road and avoid the giant pit in the highway, but we lose speed and he can't reach the gas well enough to turn us back onto the frontage road. So we drive over a black and yellow painted curb, through a small grassy patch, over another black and yellow curb, and through someone's front garden.

Sam drops her *samoon*, half eaten, down the turret and holds on with both hands. The .50's barrel cranes to the sky and bounces around as we drive a six-thousand-pound up-armored gun truck over various domestic parts of Baghdad. Two children playing soccer stop and watch with a woman on a porch as Thunder 2 faithfully follows our path over gardens and curbs through their neighborhood. When we exit the garden and are back on pavement, Flo gives the gun truck as much gas as he can, and we pick up speed for half an Iraqi block. The block we are on curves to the right and wanders down a narrowing street. The four-foot wall just left of our current path would be considered a sound barrier to the interstate on the other side if it were in Colorado or Ohio. In Baghdad, it prevents errant soccer balls from bounding into traffic and is spray-painted with an Arabic phrase I can't read and the number 38.

M1114 gun trucks have a tremendous amount of inertia and strongly resist changes in direction. When the fluid that facilitates these changes leaks out from the undercarriage, leaving dolloped slime in its wake, such changes take enormous amounts of conviction, physical strength, nerve, and split-second prioritization to achieve.

Flo stands up a little in his seat, lets off the gas, and grabs the wheel tighter still. Sam braces herself in the turret. "Wall," I say over the radio to Thunder 2. When we hit the wall just to the left of the 3 and after the words, Sam ducks and steadies herself against the extra cans of ammo we have in the back. The wall yields easily to our truck and seems to explode outward from the first point of impact like the final cymbals of a long-awaited crescendo. In the side mirror, I watch Thunder 2 bounce over the pieces in our trail. We go through a small ditch sprouting reeds and find ourselves merging into the flow of traffic on the highway, silent except for the passenger's side windshield wiper, the only one that moves. The driver's side wiper is stuck at a forty-degree angle across the short, rectangular windshield.

Sam grabs the half-eaten *samoon* off the floor of the back seat, wipes off the dirt, and stands back up in the turret. Flo cranks the wheel as hard as he can, breaking off the wiper lever, and we exit the highway onto a side street lined with the same kind of wall we just drove past. This road is known to house randomly violent anti-American residents—one of whom is alleged to have shot down the U.S. base's observation blimp in an attack disguised as a holiday celebration. The road curves to the left; we follow its path by ricocheting off another wall. Thunder 2 swerves around the debris we leave behind. As we approach our gate, Sam yells at the gate guards and motions for them to lift the beam. Instead of taking the road, we take a more direct path through an open field and the parking lot of the kebab restaurant before we reach our compound, turn off the jammers, and wait for Tonya to open the gate.

Flo parks the truck perpendicular to all the other vehicles so he does not have to turn again. Our second truck parks ninety degrees to our right. Schwab gets out and we meet at the rear of our truck for the post-mission debrief. Flo exits through his door, hands oozing blood and trembling, holding the wiper lever. Facing the wall in front of Schwab's truck, and to the right of ours, we clear our weapons and safe them. Montana and Sam start to break down and store the crew-served weapons. The rest of us take off our body armor. Sarkis laughs and walks away, jingling his MP-5 over his shoulder, and mutters "Ernest Hemingway's mom" between snickers.

We stand behind the broken-down gun truck, bled out of the fluid that makes it possible to drive in a country full of bad bridges, broken walls, and bleeding American hands. Our two closest army allies responsible for our safety on these trips, Montana and Sam, make sexual gestures with the .50 cal gun barrel and count only twelve naturally occurring "your mom" jokes from the trip. Flo looks at Schwab, says, "Fuck you, sir," throws the wiper lever at his feet, and walks away.

Schwab looks at me and shrugs. "Makes as much sense as anything else," he says. He grabs his gear and walks across a gravel pathway, past the camp's only bathroom, and around a concrete blast wall to drop his gear in his room before we meet back up for a dinner of Lucky Charms with milk that doesn't need refrigeration and never expires.

This is my third day in Iraq.

2

Fly Fishing

WHEN I ARRIVED HERE IN FEBRUARY, BRIAN, THE GUY I replaced, took me aside and told me Sarkis, his interpreter, knows everything, that I don't have to worry while I'm here, just trust Sarkis. Sarkis's father is someone fairly high up in either the Lebanese government or military, and their family owns a considerable amount of land up in the hills outside of Beirut. He has been working for the army unit I am attached to for almost four years. He isn't a U.S. citizen, Brian told me, but he's close. Brian said all he's waiting on is a trip back to Boston, where he lived before he started working here, to take the Oath of Allegiance.

Later that first day, Sarkis took me aside and told me Brian didn't really know what was going on and preferred to go out to the trash pile and shoot pen flares at birds. It's been three weeks since Brian and his team left Iraq and Brian went back to his life in Missouri.

Every Saturday Sarkis and I have tea together in my office before we go to meet the Iraqis I advise on logistics of international counterterrorism. And every Saturday he brings me a gift. The first Saturday, it was a tea set. There are ten cups in the set, five pairs, each pair with a different color glass that forms the rim of the cup and the outermost part of the saucer. The teapot is a glass amalgamation of all the colors of the cups and saucers. The second Saturday, it was another pair of shackles and handcuffs—with no key—that he demanded I keep in my desk drawer with the others and a small plaster bust of Saddam Hussein. Then there was a ride in a motorcycle sidecar around the palaces on

Camp Victory, another lighter that projected Saddam's face, a stack of bootlegged movies (which he evidently didn't screen, as half of them were porn), a poster of some Lebanese celebrity I didn't know, a map of Iraq split in two and taped back together, a pair of the underwear the Iraqi commandos are issued (still in its "Made in USA" packaging), and an ivory revolver mounted on red velvet in a wooden frame. Today he comes to my office for tea and gives me a giant sword mounted on a piece of dark wood and etched with "Xena Warrior Princess," some Arabic I can't read, and the number 77.

"Where did you get this?" I ask him.

"From my sources," Sarkis says as he adds sugar to the tiny teacups.

"Who are your sources?" I ask him.

"Did you know that I once worked at the Pentagon?" he says. "I had a six-month contract. It was only six months because of the nature of the work. It was very classified."

"Did you bring Brian gifts on Saturdays?" I ask.

Sarkis stirs his tea and flips through the green hardback notebook Brian left me.

"When are you going back to Boston for that oath?" I ask him.

"Soon," he says, "when things cool off here a bit and I can afford to be gone. I know how important my work as a counterterrorism adviser is here. I don't want to jeopardize it."

"You're an interpreter," I say. "I'm the adviser."

"You would be interested in the work I did at the Pentagon," he says. "But as you know, I can't talk about it. And Brian was already married."

Today we have a meeting with the general in charge of the unit of Iraqis we advise. The U.S. government brought him to power a decade ago when he and his Kurdish countrymen agreed to fight with the United States against Saddam. He rose quickly through the Iraqi ranks and now commands nearly three thousand Iraqi Special Operations soldiers. He is a short man, maybe five feet seven, a few inches shorter than I am, and speaks quietly. His deputy, Hussein, is the voice of the unit and does most of the yelling. Sarkis told me about today's meeting on Thursday, adding that General Fadhil specifically requested it.

After we finish our tea, we walk out to the car to drive to Fadhil's office. I have a car of my own, a plum-colored Trailblazer that gets three radio stations: Hayati FM, the Armed Forces Radio, and one that only plays someone wailing verses of the Quran on Fridays. Sarkis has a car too, but it is not U.S. issued. It's a white Toyota Hilux truck that was reportedly a gift from Fadhil. Sarkis prefers to drive his truck, and Brian didn't mind. I tell him I like the air conditioning better in the Blazer and insist on driving. He stops by his truck and grabs a box of mint mojito hookah he imports for some of the Iraqi commandos. They have hookah together every night and Sarkis invites me often. I go once a week and drink tea while the men smoke mint mojito–, pink bubble gum–, and cotton candy–flavored tobacco under a tent next to a kebob restaurant. Sarkis has taught me how to order my own chai with half the normal amount of sugar: *chai, chai, shukar hafif*. He hasn't been able to explain why I have to say chai twice.

When we pull up to Fadhil's office, Sarkis hands the hookah box to the guy who waters the sidewalk every morning. "He's just cleaning it," Sarkis tells me when I ask him what the man is doing, but as he stands there watering with a too-short garden hose and unusually low water pressure, it looks like he is just watering the concrete, which is wet every day we come to this building. We pass Hussein's office on our way to the general. Hussein comes out to greet us and invites us into his office for tea. He shakes my hand with both of his and kisses both my cheeks. Sarkis has started to time how long Hussein holds onto my hands when we meet. The record is forty-seven seconds. As we have tea with Hussein, Sarkis rearranges the chess pieces on his green jade and black onyx chess set. They have a conversation that Sarkis does not interpret for me, and then we get up to leave and shake hands. Thirty-nine seconds.

General Fadhil's office is the largest room in this concrete building. His desk sits at the very back and is flanked by a decorative stone globe and a table covered in knives. One of them appears to have dried blood on it. On the wall, to the left of his desk, is a collection of seventeen Kalashnikovs, each with a different attachment: a suppressor, a single scope optic, an extra-large-capacity magazine, a makeshift bayonet, something I cannot identify. Some of them appear to be loaded. Hanging above the door is a rug featuring a fiercely glaring Native American woman holding a wolf with bared teeth; behind them, a crescent moon glows. A flat-screen TV streams live news between the wolf wall hanging and the gun collection. Red couches line the walls, and on the right of his desk, near the globe, is a high-backed gold velvet chair. This is where I sit when we come in. Sarkis sits on a couch to my right and takes out a notebook and pen, signs he intends to interpret the meeting.

Fadhil, one of the most lethal men in this country during the last ten years, shakes my hand gently with a limp wrist and sits down. He says something to Sarkis, who nods, gets up, and takes three small chocolates wrapped in orange foil off a table in the center of the room. We eat the chocolates while the chai boy makes chai in the galley outside. Fadhil begins to say something to Sarkis. Unlike many other Iraqis we work with, Fadhil has a fairly American way of doing business. He has tea as a cultural formality but would prefer to only discuss work. Sarkis jots down some notes, asks a few questions, and gestures to something behind Fadhil with one hand, then both hands. Both men nod, and Sarkis takes a few more notes.

"He says that they need more cleaning kits for their weapons. And some more lubricant. They've been using gasoline," Sarkis says to me and continues the discussion with the general. The chai boy—whom everyone calls the chai boy but who is almost fifty—comes in carrying a silver platter of chai cups. Fadhil takes one, I take one, Sarkis takes one. As I begin to stir the sugar, Fadhil shoots his chai like a shot of cheap tequila. Sarkis follows suit. Both men stand up and shake hands. Sarkis looks at me while I set down my half-consumed tea, shake Fadhil's limp hand, and walk out.

"This is bullshit," Sarkis says as we walk down the hall and back to the car. "I'll show you."

We get in the car and Sarkis tells me to drive away from the U.S. section of this Iraqi base, toward the maintenance build-ings and the power plant that provides intermittent power to the Iraqis we live with, not because it lacks capacity, but because the Iraqis prefer to not turn it all the way on and instead use the U.S.-funded gasoline for their own cars. We pass the farthest mainte-nance building and keep driving on the paved road, neatly lined with a black and yellow striped curb. When we reach the end of the pavement, Sarkis points me toward a dirt road. We drive through ruts that have dried under the Iraqi sun to form deep, sharp channels in the mud.

"Stop here," Sarkis says as we near the edge of the trash pile.

I park and we exit the car. I knew the trash pile was here because sometimes we come out here, with a liter of diesel and an incen-diary grenade, to dispose of classified information with an accel-erant and 4,500 degrees of white phosphorus. But Sarkis leads me down a footpath I've not noticed in my two previous trips to the far side of this ten-foot-deep pit in the earth.

"Look," he says and points to the ground. Under my feet are what look like long, rusting caterpillars. He reaches down and grabs a handful of dirty, sunbaked pipe cleaners. We walk farther along and he stops to pick up a handful of small cotton patches held together with mud. "We bought them cleaning kits three years ago. A few thousand of them. And look where they are. So much waste, and then he asks for more!" Sarkis stomps out of the pit and stands on its rim looking west, where dark birds circle over-head. I kick the dirt around for a while to see what else has been discarded and baked into the earth outside of Baghdad. There are small bottles of gun cleaner, their labels bleached white. Tan car-rying cases with rusting metal clips bundled together in stacks of twenty. Brushes for 9mm pistols, long rifles, crew-served weapons. A few yards farther north is a pile of at least fifty boots with faded tags still on them, half buried under sand-infused T-shirts spilling out of packages that faintly say "Made in USA" on them.

Sarkis yells something from the rim of the trash pile, and I make my way out of the pit to where he stands. He's on the near bank of a canal yelling at some Iraqi commandos holding a net on the far side.

"What are they doing?" I ask Sarkis.

"Fishing," he says and points to the net. The net is circular with rocks tied into the rim as weights. The men throw it into the canal, which runs into this base from Abu Ghraib, watch as it sinks, then quickly pull a string that closes the net into a sphere. Then they haul it out of the canal hoping for fish. The first man does not catch any and gives the net to another man, who spreads it out before he throws it like a Frisbee back into the canal. When he hauls it out, the net is empty again. Sarkis yells something at the men. A third man tries the net, but he too does not catch any fish. Sarkis snickers. The fourth man bends down and takes something out of his bag.

"Cover your ears," Sarkis tells me and jams his index fingers into his own.

The fourth man unpins a grenade and throws it into the water. An explosive bubble erupts from the canal, and slowly five or six fish float to the surface. The first man uses a pool skimmer to extract them from the waves. Sarkis laughs and turns to walk back to the car. "They're not even good fish," he says.

I SIT UNDER THE CAMOUFLAGE-NETTED CANOPY WITH Schwab, who advises the other brigade of Iraqi commandos who operate from the regional outstations across the country. He is also—despite not having any relevant training, and it not being entirely legal for him to obligate government money—responsible for a contract worth a few million U.S. dollars. In the month we've been here, he has figured out that the contract is with some Dutch company called No Lemon to modify a bunch of HMMWVs for the Iraqis. Pete, the guy Schwab replaced, evidently did not do anything with the contract, and instead courted an Iraqi woman named Julie whom he occasionally smuggled into U.S. dining facilities for dinners in exchange for sexual favors later, in his room or car. Pete also used the government email account Schwab now uses to arrange their meetings. For the first two weeks we were here, Schwab thought Julie was somehow involved with the contract. When she told him she would not give him a blowjob without cake, Schwab left her outside the gate of a U.S. base and came back to tell me about her.

"Pete called her 'The Source,'" Schwab says to me. "I called the number listed as 'The Source' in the phone he gave me and she answered. Said if I took her to the barbecue buffet at Liberty on Wednesday she'd fuck me. Ride me like a cowboy, she said."

"Better be good barbecue," I say.

"You get anything weird in your phone?" he asks me.

"Just some messages from Brian's wife. Mostly about their kid starting to walk and how much she missed him."

"Nothing sexy?"

"I deleted all of them when I realized who they were from."

"I don't think my wife would fuck me if all I did was bring her cake," he says.

We sit on the benches under this canopy, early in the morning, and sip coffee I make from a French press my mom sent me from a Starbucks in Albuquerque. In March in Iraq, the mornings are crisp and pleasant. The sunlight feels kind, and it doesn't seem so far-fetched that civilization might have started here. My phone rings in my pocket, playing some Arabic tune I cannot change because all the settings are in Arabic. I learned to identify Arabic numbers from the keypad of this phone, and Sarkis has taken the time to teach me how to count when we go out for hookah and chai. The number appears in Arabic, and I answer.

"Hello," I say.

"*Alo, Jameela!*" says the voice on the other end, followed by a nervous laugh. I know from the voice and the nervous laugh that it is Major Hadi. Hadi runs the Iraqi anti-hijacking unit out of the Baghdad International Airport. He's never had a woman as an adviser before, and every time we meet he whispers things to Sarkis and laughs nervously. Hadi has a small gap between his front teeth through which he blows a rectangular stream of Camel cigarette smoke. The first time we met, he offered me a cigarette, thought better of it, took it back, then felt bad for taking it back and gave me the whole pack. I smiled and said no, thank you, and returned it. He put the pack back in the left top pocket of his uniform shirt, laughed nervously, and wrung his hands until Sarkis said something to him that made him relax.

On that first visit, Major Hadi asked for my phone number, which I gave him. Sometimes he calls me, even though he doesn't really speak English and I don't really speak Arabic. Most of the other men I work with call Sarkis when they need something from me, but Hadi insists on calling me directly, and every time he does, he asks for *Naqueeb Jameela*—Captain Beautiful, the name all the Iraqis call me—then he laughs nervously until I can find someone who speaks Arabic.

"*Jameela! Jameela! Alo, asalaam aleykum!*"

"*Aleykum asalaam, saydie,*" I say. "Hello, sir." Besides the numbers from zero to one hundred, this is almost all the Arabic I know. I walk about the compound until I find an interpreter who can talk to Hadi for me. Francis, Schwab's interpreter, happens to be watching soccer and eating Coco Puffs in the morale trailer. I hand him the phone and wait while they have a conversation. Francis ends the conversation and hands the phone back to me.

"Can you show me how to program his name with his number?" I ask Francis, who takes the phone back, does something, and returns the phone with Major Hadi's name programmed to his number. In Arabic.

"You are to meet Major Hadi for lunch and to discuss something very important," Francis says as I look at the phone. "Would you like me to go and interpret for you?" Francis is a local national interpreter, meaning he is from Baghdad. He and his family live on this base with the Iraqi soldiers.

"If I can't find Sarkis, I'll let you know," I say. Francis turns and walks away from me. The local nationals resent Sarkis because he is friends with many of the commandos, because Fadhil gave him a car, because in Lebanese Arabic you say *quifack* for "how are you" instead of the Baghdadi *schlonick*, because he keeps an MP-5 9mm machine gun in his room illegally, because he tells all the Iraqis that he is better than the LNs, because Americans are not occupying his country. The other interpreters, who are U.S. citizen interpreters from places like Deerfield, Michigan, and Bakersfield, California, mostly ignore Sarkis because they have already taken the oath.

I walk out of the morale trailer and back to Schwab, who is talking to Sarkis on the bench.

"You knew about The Source?" Schwab asks Sarkis as I walk up.

"Of course I can't tell you about what I did for the Pentagon," Sarkis says and winks at Schwab.

"We have a meeting with Major Hadi over lunch," I say to Sarkis. "You have to come," I say to Schwab.

WE SHOULDN'T BE ALLOWED TO DRIVE THE PLUM TRAIL-blazer to the meeting with the anti-hijacking unit, because we have to drive miles through Baghdad to get there, and the Blazer has no radio, no GPS tracker, and no armor. When I talk to them about the best driving route to the unit, our counterintelligence guys mention that Hadi's unit is made up largely of Iraqis who wanted to be commandos but couldn't pass the U.S. vetting process. But because the unit is stationed near the Baghdad International Airport, they never have to enter U.S.-guarded territory. We make the final turn to meet Hadi and his men, passing a heap of destroyed vehicles that commemorate the U.S. occupation of the airport with a mangled sculpture of bombed, burned, and battered buses and Jetway stairs once used to help passengers out of airplanes. I've only been out here twice before, so Sarkis still has to tell me where to turn. Schwab sits in the back seat and looks at an incoming Russian cargo plane that looks like it is going too slow to fly.

"It's like flying Moby Dick," Schwab says.

"Moby Dick." Sarkis snickers.

We pull into the compound, which is a collection of concrete buildings brightly painted maroon, gold, and green. Lined up on the sidewalk, standing on the black and yellow striped curb, are men from Hadi's unit, waiting to greet us. We park and Hadi opens my door.

"*Jameela! Jameela!*" he greets me and laughs nervously after he shakes my hand. Schwab and Sarkis get out and walk with us to a concrete building that serves as their dining hall. Sitting on three upside-down trash-can lids are a half dozen fish that look swollen and have missing patches of scales and incomplete dorsal fins. Schwab pokes one of the fish as Hadi explains something to Sarkis.

"He wants you to tour their buildings. All of them, before lunch," Sarkis interprets as Hadi nods along with the English words. I nod in Hadi's direction, and he claps his hands and smiles widely before waving me along behind him.

"This is one of the dorms," Sarkis interprets as we walk into one of the rooms. A single light bulb hangs from the ceiling, an exposed copper wire powering it and running directly into the outlet, with no plug. The bedrolls are on the floor, and outside is a ladder to the roof.

"Because we have no air conditioners or beds, sometimes my soldiers sleep on the roof," Hadi says to me. The four men who share this room stand proudly next to their wall lockers, adorned with posters of Cristiano Ronaldo and Lionel Messi, and smile when I look at them.

"Why don't you have air conditioners or beds?" I ask him.

He explains something to Sarkis, who interprets, "Because the last adviser forgot about us, and the battalion commander didn't give us any. But Brian didn't exactly forget about them. We came out here once and found the motorcycle and sidecar. We wanted to drive it around, but it wouldn't start. Something bad with the starter or maybe the oil. But I got it fixed for us to ride around. Still wasn't quite right though."

"So why don't they have air conditioners or beds?" I ask Sarkis.

Hadi leads us into another concrete room that looks almost identical, except for the posters of football players decorating lockers. We walk into their team room, the room where they assemble for training, missions if need be, and day-to-day operations. Maps of the airfield are overlaid with transparencies of various colors indicating different response zones and marking areas best suited for particular linear takedown tactics. Their company's sergeant major stands by the maps and explains things that Sarkis doesn't interpret for me. Halfway through the explanation of purple concentric circles, he stops, looks at Hadi, who looks at Sarkis, and waits for him to interpret.

"That's the purple zone," Sarkis says. "I think we'll have to have lunch with them, and I don't think they have a bakery. I can show you where to buy whiskey and good Cuban cigars on the way home if you want. I know the guy well and he gave Brian good discounts."

To my left, Schwab is tracing cracks in the concrete with his finger. We leave the team room, without an explanation of what the rest of the map shows us, and walk back to the dining hall, which is a patio between the team room and one of the dorms. White plastic tables and chairs are flaking from their exposure to the sun. Hadi shows us to the table, where we sit down.

"*Saydie*," I say to him, "where do you get your food and cook it?" Sarkis interprets to Hadi.

"When they can, the support unit where we live brings their food out here in transportable hot containers. When that can't happen, they have a propane burner in the back and improvise their kitchen equipment. Today, they went to a special bakery that makes the best *samoon* in Baghdad. We're having that and fish."

Samoon has quickly become my favorite element of Iraqi meals.

25

I often want to bite a corner, fill it with honey, and share New Mexican sopapilla technique with an Iraqi.

One of Hadi's soldiers brings in a basket filled with the freshly made *samoon*, places it in front of me, and smiles. A second soldier brings in a trash-can lid full of spiced rice, slightly burned on the bottom. A third soldier brings in the fish, cooked whole on the trash-can lid and stuffed with some spices I don't recognize. The last soldier brings in the chai and passes it out before sitting down to eat with us. Hadi takes a large knife off the table and chops the fish into portions he gives out on paper plates decorated with red maple leaves. Like most meals I have had with the Iraqis, there are no utensils. We take scoops of the rice in our hands and put it on our plates while the bread gets passed around in baskets. Hadi looks around the table, at his soldiers, at me, and then smiles. He waves his hand like he is presenting the grand prize in a game show and says, "*Alo, Jameela, alo*, thank you, thank you, *alo!*"

I nod, and we start eating. The bread is soft and lightly salted. I eat scoopfuls of the rice using pieces of bread as spoons and pick at the lemony fish, pulling pin bones out of my mouth and setting them down on the maple-leafed plates. We sip chai and listen as the Iraqis talk about football, which I recognize only by the Champions League club names. One of the soldiers looks at me and asks, "Barcelona? Madrid?" I appreciate the fact they seem to know I like soccer, even though I have never discussed having played in college or having coached a high school team when I was in grad school. To some of my fellow Americans here, my love for soccer makes me less American. To Hadi's men, it makes me more relatable. Of the two Spanish teams, I pick Barcelona, though I have no particularly favorite La Liga team. This pleases half the group and upsets the other half. We pass around another basket of *samoon*.

I look at Hadi, who looks at me and smiles after each bite he takes. He avoids eye contact with Sarkis throughout the meal. I watch Schwab eat for a bit and notice he spends a long time chewing and has no pin bones on his plate. He looks me straight in the eye as I pull a bone out of my mouth and looks at his own plate and keeps chewing. Hadi says something to Sarkis, who finishes his bite and interprets, "Can you find them beds and air conditioners?"

"I'll try, *saydie*," I say to Hadi, who smiles again and nods as Sarkis interprets for him.

After the meal, Hadi offers me a cigarette, blushes remembering I refused the last time, and bows repeatedly. He takes a small piece of paper out and writes something in Arabic on it. It looks like a single word, but all Arabic still looks like ornate squiggles to me. He hands me the paper, points at Sarkis, who has his back to me and is talking to Schwab, and shakes his index finger back and forth. He drags an index finger across his throat in what I perceive as the universal sign for murder. He senses the panic in my glance, points to Sarkis again, shakes his head back and forth vigorously, saying, "*La, la, la,*" no, no no, and points to the paper again. I nod, take the paper, and put it into my pocket.

Sarkis turns around as a soldier brings one last round of chai, which we drink at the long table in the grass between Hadi's buildings. Sarkis says something to Hadi, who nods and comes to shake my hand. He grabs it with both of his hands then lets go with his left hand, laughs nervously, says, "*Shukran, Jameela,*" and walks us to the car. We get in and drive off as Hadi and his men smile and wave at us from the black and yellow striped curb.

"You want that whiskey?" Sarkis asks.

"Not really," I say. I turn up the radio, which is tuned to Hayati FM.

"This is Fares Karam," Sarkis says. "He's Lebanese. All the good pop stars are Lebanese. I have his album. I'll give it to you."

WHEN IT RAINS IN IRAQ, MUD CLINGS TO EVERYTHING. IT sucks boots off feet, it bonds to the fabric of pants, and it fills the wheel wells of HMMWVs responding to indirect fire so they stop

27

rolling. Insurgent mud. Mud that makes the air smell like a pottery room full of unfired sculpture, the kiln a few months away.

There is no drainage on our compound so lakes form. All the decking we've walked on for two months finally makes sense, except now it is coated in a thin, invisible layer of the slippery insurgent mud. Anyone who walks the decking to avoid the lakes risks an insurgent mud–induced fall. Yesterday, right after the big storm, Sarkis convinced some of the fishing commandos to give him a small live fish (caught with the net, not the grenade), which he added to the giant lake by the front door of our compound. Schwab and I sit under the canopy and watch the fish swim around in seven or eight inches of water.

"You could give it to The Source when it dies," I say. "I wonder what that would get you."

"Herpes, probably," Schwab says.

Sarkis walks up to us and sits down. As soon as he sits down, he stands back up. "We have to go see Fadhil," he says.

"It's Friday," Schwab says. Friday is the holy day in Iraq and our only day off.

"Let's go," Sarkis says to me. He waves to the fish as we walk out.

I walk toward the Trailblazer, which sits in five or six inches of muddy water.

"I have to drive," Sarkis says.

I put the keys back in my pocket and find the paper Hadi gave me. I hand it to Sarkis.

"What's this say?"

He turns the paper right side up, reads it, and hands it back to me.

"Trust," he says. "Where did you get it?"

"I found it on the ground by the lake," I tell him as we get into his Hilux, which smells like sweat, gasoline, and hookah smoke.

We drive to Fadhil's office. The parking lot is empty except for his up-armored SUV and now Sarkis's truck. We get out and walk across the sidewalks, which today, after a storm that dropped almost half the annual rain, are completely dry. We walk into the dark building, past Hussein's empty office, past the empty galley where the chai boy prepares chai, into Fadhil's office, which is lit only by the sunlight spilling in from the window behind him. The general sits in his desk chair and strokes his mustache as we enter. He stands up when we walk to him, hugs Sarkis, kisses both of his cheeks, and shakes his hand. He looks at me and bows. He says something to Sarkis, who nods, looks at the ground, and nods again. Fadhil takes a large brown envelope off his desk and empties the contents into his hand. He counts out 2,500 U.S. dollars in hundred-dollar bills and gives them to Sarkis. We leave.

In the car ride back to the U.S. compound, Sarkis tells me he has to leave Iraq tomorrow. "Can you take me to the airport?"

"You going back to do the oath?" I ask him.

"What oath?" he asks and turns up the radio.

I look out the window as we arrive back on our side of the base. He puts the car in park but doesn't turn it off.

"I have to take care of a few things," he says.

I nod, get out of the car, and ask, "What time tomorrow?"

WE SHOULDN'T BE ALLOWED TO DRIVE A FLATBED TRUCK full of old bed frames, mattresses, and fans to the airport to drop off Sarkis, principally because neither Schwab, whom I made come with me, nor I is qualified to drive this truck. But my friends at the air base were getting rid of these beds, and we went to pick them up and take them to Hadi and his men, which I figured could best happen early on Saturday morning after I drop off Sarkis at the airport. Sarkis sits in the back with his luggage and the bed frames.

"You couldn't have fucking waited a few hours to bring the beds?" he asks. He points out where I need to turn to get to Hadi's unit, and we turn the other direction to go to the Bagdad International Airport passenger terminal. Armed men from the Iraqi army and the Ministry of Interior line the yellow and black striped curb as we pull in. They stare at us. One of the men raises his weapon to the low ready. Sarkis jumps out and starts yelling at him, and he lowers his gun at once. Sarkis walks around to my window. I lower it to shake his hand. He hands me Fares Karam's CDs, a stack of papers he thinks I will find useful, and a pen flare.

"Good luck, *Jameela*," he says. "You too, Schwab."

From the passenger seat Schwab salutes him casually with his index and middle finger. Sarkis turns around and walks toward the terminal.

3

God Willing

THE IRAQI FIRE STATION IS JUST ON THE OTHER SIDE OF the concrete blast walls, to our west, that divide the U.S. compound from the rest of the Iraqi base we live on. They have three rescue pumpers and an ambulance parked at the hospital, which sits on the east side of our twelve-foot-high blast-protected perimeter. Today I have to ask Hisham for a tour of the fire station because Perry, the Green Beret commander I work for, wants to know if the Iraqis respond to our fire emergencies. I don't know the answer, because I don't know how to alert the fire station of such an emergency.

Hisham is reluctant at first to bring me to his fire station. Hameed, my new interpreter, told me after our last meeting with him that Hisham is worried no one here is looking after me. Hameed is from Bakersville, California, and grew up in Baghdad. He thinks Hisham is concerned because, when I go see him, I am alone with Hameed and because I am the first woman to be his American adviser.

Hisham is a big rectangular man, slightly balding, with curly black hair. Because he talks only out of the right side of his mouth, his words move his black mustache asymmetrically. He is in charge of the unit that maintains this installation, so I know that he is my most important Iraqi. But all our sporadic interactions so far have been random American requests from me and expressions of fatherly concern from him. "Maybe you should buy him something nice," Hameed suggests.

When Hisham finally agrees to take me to the fire station, we walk from his office to the building just north of his headquarters, where I meet Ali, the fire chief. He welcomes me to the station, and before inviting me in for chai, he asks me to buy him a truck, painted red with lights on top, that says "Fire Chief" on the side. "I don't know how to say 'Fire Chief' in Arabic," I say.

"He wants it in English," Hameed interprets.

Inside the station, Hisham walks me around the common area, a large table with mismatched chairs and a map of the base under a piece of glass that is not the same shape as the table. The portion of the base walled off by towering concrete, where I live with a few dozen other Americans, is solid black. In the rest of the base, where four thousand Iraqis and their families live, roads, street names, and speed bumps are carefully marked. After Hisham shows me the map, we drink chai and walk outside the station to where the three rescue pumpers are parked neatly in a row, facing out, poised for a rapid exit. Hisham maintains his vehicles better than any other unit on this base. He does weekly inspections and tells me he knows how to drive any one of them, from the fire engine to the water truck, even the crane. The water trucks are separated into categories: The blue trucks hold potable water; the tan trucks hold wastewater. Sarah, the only other woman here (besides me) and my plumber, told me she spent two and a half weeks dissuading the Iraqi plumbers from trying to weld a bulkhead into each of these trucks and hold potable water on one side of the bulkhead and wastewater on the other.

"Efficiency," they told her, because they would need only one truck to service the buildings.

"Severe illness," Sarah told them.

Eventually, they abandoned their efficient idea. Not because of Sarah's advice but because they didn't have enough material to properly weld the bulkheads. Standing next to a truck that, instead of water, stores some of the tools the plumbers use infrequently, I ask Hisham how their fire response works. Ali steps in to explain the process. "When we see a fire, we call someone on that part of the base that we know and ask if there really is a fire and if they need help. If they say yes, we go."

"What happens if you can't get a hold of anyone on that part of the base?" I ask.

"We guess," he says, "and if they need us, we'll be there, *insha'allah*."

Hisham nods; by now I know that means he is tired of the conversation. He motions us back to his office for chai before he asks Hameed if I am all right and if someone is taking care of me. Hameed shrugs and says something he doesn't explain to me later, and Hisham dismisses us.

I report my findings to Perry. "If they see something that looks like a fire, they call someone they know on that part of the base to confirm it. If they don't get a hold of anyone, they guess," I say.

"Well, fuck," he says. "These are the people you work with?"

Perry is on his seventh deployment to this location. He has known the Iraqi commandos he works with for almost nine years. He has done missions, raided buildings, killed people, dragged targets out of their houses in the middle of the night, and interrogated targets side by side with the Iraqis we live with. He has been consumed with training the Iraqis on counterterrorism tactics for nearly a decade. Never in the past nine years has he been concerned with their fire response. Until now, when his job as commander is to make the Iraqis ready for our exit from this country. His concerns are now almost the same as mine. How do they get bullets? Who runs the hospital? Where does their electricity come from? How do they call 9-1-1? (They don't.)

"He's the best one I have," I say.

"Well, fuck," he says.

"HISHAM WOULD LIKE YOU TO HELP HIM INSPECT THE SOLdiers' dorms," Hameed comes to tell me a few days later as I eat a mixture of Cheerios and Lucky Charms. Under the blowing AC unit in our office trailer, which displays the temperature with the increasing size of snowflakes, I sip the Piñon coffee my mom sends me from Albuquerque and I make in the French press, which I haven't washed in four months. Despite it already being triple digits, midmorning hot coffee is one of the few things that make sense here. I keep my coffee stash in the top drawer of this desk, along with the beige washcloth I use to wipe yesterday's grounds out of the press every morning at 8:30 before I make a new batch; a few paperclips; some dried-up Wite-Out; a collection of semi-functional government-issued pens; and the Saddam lighter.

"*Schwakit?*" I say, practicing my Arabic. Hazbar, one of the battalion directors of logistics, and Ahmed, the brigade director of logistics, try to teach me Arabic during our morning meetings. Over chai every morning, they give me a new phrase. We started with the most essential: *insha'allah*, which literally means "God willing" but is used, more or less ubiquitously, to describe something that needs to be done but that no one wants to do, and most likely won't be done by an Iraqi.

"*Saydie*, will you have the generator fixed in time for dinner?"

"*Insha'allah.*" (All the mechanics but one are on leave, and the one that is here doesn't work before 9:00 p.m.)

"*Saydie*, will you be at the meeting in Balad tomorrow?"

"*Insha'allah.*" (He hates the Iraqi general in charge of the meeting and has lent his car to someone on base whose name he cannot recall.)

I have finally learned how to use this phrase for myself.

"Will there be more money for new air conditioners?" Hameed interprets for me in a meeting with Hazbar.

"*Insha'allah*," I say to Hazbar.

"Hazbar wants to know if that is Iraqi *insha'allah* or American *insha'allah*," Hameed interprets.

Everyone knows the difference.

So far, other than *insha'allah*, I have now learned to count to a thousand, and Hazbar and Ahmed have each taught me what he considers his second most useful phrase. From Ahmed, I have learned *schwakit tinsel?* When do you go on leave? From Hazbar: *wen el ratib malta?* Where is my paycheck? Hameed has taught

me *schwakit aerja?* When do you come back? I've also learned
to recognize *mushkila, maku mushkila,* and *mushkila kirbala*—
problem, no problem, and very big problem. Hisham has never
tried to teach me Arabic.

I watch as steam rises off my coffee, even in the summer heat,
and chase a lone Cheerio around the bowl. "In like twenty minutes," Hameed says as he holds up his cell phone in his left hand
and shakes it like he's mixing a can of spray paint before use.
Though he's my third interpreter, after Sarkis and a brief period
with a guy named Daniel, who was flown back to the United States
after he started going blind in one eye, I've been with Hameed
long enough to know that the spray paint cell phone shake means
Hisham has called him. He fears Hisham almost as much as Hisham's own men do. His men run the dining facility, the power plant,
the U.S.-funded Reverse Osmosis Water Purification Unit, which
has been working for three months but hasn't been used yet, the
gym, the barbershop, and the soldiers' dorms. They also run the
fire department, hospital, and trash service. Hisham wears the
same electric-blue jumpsuits he issues to his mechanics because
he finds it important to relate to his soldiers. He invites me to do
dorm inspections because he finds it important to demonstrate
how organized, neat, and professional his soldiers are.

His men are not part of the commando units in this brigade
that Perry works with. They are the support soldiers that make
it possible for the commandos to eat, bathe, sleep in air conditioning, have electricity, and drink clean water (soon from the
ROWPU, *insha'allah*). But like us—their American advisers in
charge of logistics, sustainment, and support—the commandos
look down on them for not being on the teams that kick in doors
and roll up bad guys. The condescension lasts until the power
goes out or the air conditioning cuts off. Then the commandos
beg and plead and make lunatic promises about gifts they will
bring back from missions as long as their power and air conditioning and televisions come back on first.

I've done one dorm inspection with Hisham before today. That time, we walked through four different dorms, housing almost all his three hundred support soldiers. The dorms were very neat and brightly lit and reeked overpoweringly of the Iraqi air freshener that smells of sweetly fermented despair and makes your eyes water. Each room housed between four and twelve mechanics, electricians, and plumbers, depending on size. The rooms were split by allegiances to FC Barcelona and Real Madrid, with the Real fans usually closer to the door. The electricians, Hisham told me, have the best taste, which we can discern from the presence of their pink floral bedspreads. We made note of fans with the plugs removed and copper wire diked to the loose ends—extending, fully exposed, into the wall sockets and held in place with electrical tape. Instead of alerting Hisham to this unsafe practice, which we noted in at least three rooms, I pointed to the wire and said "*mushkila*." Hameed further explained to one occupant in each room that this could be a fire hazard and made them promise to fix it. "It'll be done by this afternoon, *insha'allah*," they said.

While Hameed relayed the message, Hisham had me walk through their bathrooms, which smelled equally of the air freshener and pink urinal cakes. He made a point of showing me that his soldiers had dried the floors of the showers and the basins of the sinks. Then we left the building.

All the rocks on the path between the dorms were spray-painted orange and arranged in order by size. The rock line to my right had the biggest rocks near the door we were exiting and the smallest by the door we were approaching. The rock line to my left was the reverse, having the largest rocks at the door we approached and the smallest rocks at the door we exited. There were no weeds. "That is how much detail his men care about," Hameed interpreted for me as we walked along the orange-lined trail between two dorms.

And it's true. Their dining halls are the cleanest ones I have seen in Iraq, and this includes at least nine American contractor–run facilities and one run by the Iraqi air force. Hisham cares about decorations. His men dust the paintings on the walls and Windex the accent mirrors. Both sides of the main dining hall are color coded, one orange and one lime green in motif: portraying limes, tropical frogs, and lime-colored grass. No one, not even the commandos, spills sugar on the chai stations on their way out. Everyone stacks his tray after use. The cooks Saran wrap all the kitchen equipment immediately after it has been cleaned and dried. The pantries and freezers are arranged by date and are subject to random inspection. The cost of anything mislabeled or misplaced will be deducted from the soldier's paycheck. Hisham tells me the only thing he has ever had to deduct was the cost of one fifty-pound bag of flour, two years ago, that was not moved to the top of the stack after a new shipment arrived. The soldier who failed to restack the flour was dismissed a month later for not properly cleaning and wrapping the unused backup mixer in the bakery.

I know Hisham likes to have more than one person on the inspection so, as I finish my coffee, I tell Schwab and ask Sarah if she'll go with us. Sarah lives north of San Francisco with her seven-year-old daughter, who sends her pictures of the garden she wants to plant when Sarah returns. She sent Sarah seeds to grow a poppy and a sunflower. Sarah found pots and soil for both and planted them, but they have little chance in the 130-degree Iraqi summer. Her husband reentered active duty and was stationed in Arkansas, so their daughter lived with him for a while, but then she had to return to school in Northern California, where Sarah's mom has moved in to look after her until we come home.

Yesterday, when the water line buried behind our camp broke and formed a mud marsh between our buildings and the buildings of Perry's unit, Aaron, the U.S. Special Forces guy in charge of their camp, came to ask her for help. She agreed and went to gather a few things: a stack of red rags, a can of orange spray paint, some tape, a shovel, and two metal coat hangers, which she cut and bent to form dowsing rods. Air force plumbers are taught to calibrate the copper dowsing rods they use to find groundwater. She left to find the leak while Schwab and I took bets on how long it would take. "This is Iraq," he said. "They might find it in eight years, *insha'allah*."

Three hours later, Sarah and Aaron came back wearing suits of mud and smiles. "She's magic," Aaron told us as he explained how she used the coat hangers and walked right to the leak. She was off by only four inches when they started digging. While she found the leak, all she could do was wrap it in rags and duct tape because we didn't have a three-inch union joint to fix it with. Still, the puddle shrank by two-thirds that afternoon, which we could measure because Sarah had marked the boundaries with orange spray paint.

Sarah agrees to accompany me on the inspection if we ask Hisham for a three-inch union joint, so we each grab a clipboard and a semi-functional government-issued pen and leave with Hameed for Hisham's office. When we arrive, Hisham greets us with chai, scarves bearing their unit name and patches, and small pins displaying their unit patch. Wearing our new items, we get into the back of Hisham's SUV and depart.

"Today," Hameed interprets from the passenger's seat, "we are not going to the dorms or the dining facility or the fire station. We are going to the other areas of his unit because you have not inspected them yet. First, we will go eat bread from the bakery."

Every inspection we do begins at the bakery because Hisham is proudest of this facility. His bakers bake almost ten thousand pieces of bread a day for the people on base. Every time we come here, he shows us the mixers, the room with the chronologically arranged stack of flour bags, and the unused backup mixer, cleaned weekly, wrapped, and ready for use. After noticing that there is still no flour on the floor, we eat our bread and get back in Hisham's car. He drives us to a building I have never been in before.

"This is the gym," Hameed interprets. It is a small room that houses standard weight sets, pull-up bars, and one wall of full-length mirrors. There is also a back room with four machines that look like treadmills for small house pets and have white paw prints on the blue revolving belt. They look too flimsy for human use, but each displays a diagram of a person running, and they directly face the full-length mirrors, with less than a foot between the end of each machine and the mirror. Next to the cat treadmills are two machines with straps intended to be worn around the waist and a dial that adjusts how vigorously the strap jiggles the occupant, measured by the increasing size of a sine wave.

On the non-mirrored walls are pictures of an Iraqi bodybuilder who finished second at the Iraqi bodybuilding championships in 2007 (he's topless in the picture, save for the sash that says "Runner-up 2007" in English) and won a few years later. This champion is Omar, the soldier who runs the gym, and he shows us how he has arranged things and how each machine works, all while holding a fifty-five-pound dumbbell in his left hand. Hisham asks Schwab to test the cat treadmill. He mounts it and turns it on while Sarah and I are assigned to test the jigglers, which face the opposite direction. Hameed—who limps badly as the result of having been run over by a car in North Baghdad when he was twelve, and being denied healthcare because of his family's political ties—is exempt from testing a machine, but he tries to interpret our impressions through the purr of the treadmill and vibration of our jiggling.

"I'm getting dizzy," Schwab says to his reflection, fifteen inches away, and holds his hand over his hip-holstered pistol so it doesn't fall out during his moderate jog.

"What do-oo-ooes this ma-aa-chi-iiine do-ooo?" Sarah asks, and Hameed interprets.

"It builds ab muscles and makes you thin," Omar the bodybuilder says and switches hands with the weight to lift his shirt and rub his washboard stomach.

Hisham asks if we are finished with our inspection, and while the gym manager shows Schwab how to stop the cat treadmill, Sarah and I dismount the jiggle machines and make notes on our clipboards. We thank the manager, shake hands, and leave with Hisham to walk the orange rock–lined path to an adjacent building.

"This is the barbershop," Hameed interprets. There are two barbers, two barber chairs, and a small TV playing Real Madrid highlights hanging in the corner. Hisham asks us to notice there is no hair on the floor and asks our opinion of the decorations, which consist mainly of Real Madrid posters, player cards, and shelves adorned with porcelain statues of animals found in Africa. On the far wall hangs a poster that says, in neon-yellow letters, "THE MOST TRENDIEST WOMEN'S HAIRSTYLES EVER" and depicts a half dozen men with modest mohawks, buzz cuts, and military hairstyles. Sarah takes a picture of the poster. Hisham tells us these men are brothers, both commandos who were injured and can no longer be commandos but are now the barbers and continue to serve honorably. They both bow to Hisham as he says this. We thank them for letting us inspect their area before we get back in Hisham's car, and he drives us to his office.

"What was the best one?" Hameed interprets as Hisham sits down in his high-back chair and strokes his mustache.

Sarah, Schwab, and I discuss. Schwab believes the gym was the worst, because I made him run on a cat treadmill. I believe the gym was the best for this very reason. Sarah thinks the barbershop should win because of the poster. I ask Hameed what he thinks.

"I think he wants the barbers to win," Hameed says.

"*Saydie*," I say and Hameed interprets, "they are all excellent facilities. We can tell your soldiers are proud of what they do and are happy to be in your unit."

Hisham dips his head in agreement and mumbles to himself out of the right side of his mouth.

"But we have decided that the barbershop was the best today."

Hisham smiles and nods. He calls for more chai. Sarah reminds Hameed to ask about the three-inch union joint. Hameed nods. Hisham smiles and tells Hameed something about the barbershop. After we drink our chai, Hisham dismisses us and thanks us for helping him.

We get in our car and drive back to the U.S. part of the base. "Hisham said he would be honored if the Americans got their hair cut at the barbershop," Hameed says. "I told him someone would. He said in the meantime he could find that part."

"No fucking way," Schwab says when I look at him.

Sarah looks horrified and shakes her head. "I don't think I want one of the most trendiest women's hairstyles," she says. "Ever."

Her hair is long, brown, and a little curly. Her daughter has the same hair, and she has a picture of them braiding each other's hair. She taped it over her bed, in her room here, next to the crayon diagrams of the garden.

I drop Schwab and Sarah off at our compound and go with Hameed back to the barbershop. "Why did you tell him someone would get their hair cut there?" I ask him.

"I don't know," Hameed says. "He just seemed so happy about that idea I thought it would be good. Plus, I think he will trust you a lot more if you do. And he said he could find that union thing."

We park the car and walk into the barbershop, where the brothers are watching soccer on the small hanging TV. Hameed explains something to them for a few moments while I run my fingers through my dark blond, chin-length hair and wonder if this war would be going better if more people were willing to try a haircut produced by two Iraqi ex-commando brothers.

I sit in the chair while one of the brothers puts the cape over me. The other points to one of the men on the poster. "*Na'am?*" he asks.

"*La! La!*" I say. No! No! Not the high and tight.

"*Na'am?*"

"*La, la, la!*"

Finally, after I reject four of the male models, Hameed says something, and the barber spins me away from the mirror, says *insha'allah*, and begins to cut. I watch as Real Madrid scores on a penalty.

My barber puts down his scissors and applies some kind of gel to my hair. Hameed looks at me, presses his lips together, and nods with bigger-than-normal eyes. The barber says something to Hameed. "He wants to know if you'll pay in U.S. dollars or in dinar."

The barber turns my chair around to face the mirror. He has

cut the left side half an inch shorter than the right and has gelled my bangs down in a comb-over. He has left me sideburn-length wisps, trimmed three inches off the rest of my hair, and fixed it behind my ears with gel.

"How much do I have to pay for this?" I ask Hameed.

"Ten dollars," Hameed says. "U.S."

I hand the barber ten dollars, he hugs me, thanks me for coming in, and walks me to the door, beaming, while his brother sweeps the hair off the floor. Hameed waits until we shut the doors of my car to laugh so hard he cries.

"Oh my God!" Schwab says as I walk through the steel door of our compound. He and Sarah are sitting on the patio under the canopy we set up to keep the sun off and the temperatures below 120 because the power is out and there is nothing else to do. The gel in my hair begins to melt as I walk toward them.

"You look like a butch mid-1990s lesbian," Schwab says and laughs so hard he drops to a knee and pounds his fist against the deck. Sarah looks at me and says nothing. I walk into the office trailer and set my clipboard down. I pour the coffee still in the press into my mug and sip it, staring out the door of the trailer at the concrete blast walls behind Schwab. He rolls over onto his back and grabs his stomach.

Sarah walks into the office. "It'll grow back," she says. *Insha'allah.*

As Schwab begins to compose himself enough to sit upright, Flo comes running through the steel front door of our compound. "The armory is on fire!" he says and points to the east, where thick black smoke is billowing over our twelve-foot-high walls. I walk outside my trailer and stare at the smoke. *Mushkila.* "What's in the armory?" I ask Flo, who is our munitions specialist and has spent his time here trying to convince the Iraqis to keep their ammunition in an area away from the family housing and behind sandbag-reinforced blast walls.

"Loose ammo, maybe grenades, C4," Flo says. *Mushkila kirbala.* Then Flo turns from the smoke to face me. "What the fuck?"

"Do we need to evacuate?" I ask him.

He moves his hand across his own hair, narrows his eyes, and clenches his teeth.

"Flo, are we in danger here?" I ask again.

"What," he says, pointing to my hair, "the fuck?"

Hameed appears by the canopy and points to the smoke. "Something's on fire," he says.

"The armory!" Schwab says, finally aware that a few million rounds of ammo, grenades, and explosive charges are cooking forty meters away from us.

Schwab's arrival in the conversation jars Flo out of his mesmerized state. "The armory!" Flo says and runs to the closest thing to a bunker we have: some concrete jersey barriers arranged to form a tunnel, topped with a sturdy board and covered in a few feet of sandbags, that butt up against the west perimeter wall. I follow him to the bunker and stand outside it. "Flo, what armory is over there?" I ask him.

He says nothing, crawls on his hands and knees farther into the bunker, and leans up against the concrete.

Around 2:00 a.m. one night, about a month ago, one of the detainees at the exploitation cell just on the southeast side of our wall escaped. Somehow word of this escaped detainee spread so quickly that in a matter of minutes Flo had woken up our entire camp, donned his body armor and helmet, and loaded his long rifle. It was on that night I discovered Flo had been making trades with some of Perry's guys to get better parts for his M-16. He had a shortened barrel. He had a pistol grip added to the hand guards. He had a green laser mounted on the side next to an optic designed for a much larger machine gun. We watched as Flo ran about our camp, beaming the green laser into corners of the wall, the lone bathroom, the makeshift bunker. Finally, Flo backed into the bunker and lay in the prone position, periodically shining the green laser across the patio. Later, we learned that the detainee had escaped only as far as the guard at the door of the exploitation cell, and only to ask for some water. Flo remained in the prone position in the bunker until 9:00 a.m., occasionally sleeping.

"I wonder if the water trucks are responding," Sarah says.

With Flo, our only expert on safe retreat distances for various munitions, comfortable in a makeshift bunker big enough for only one, Sarah, Schwab, Hameed, and I decide to go see the fire. To my knowledge, there is no armory to the east of our compound, and so far, no random rounds of ammunition have come shooting over the blast walls. There is the helicopter landing zone, the exploitation cell, the hospital, four dorms, the special warfare school headquarters, gun ranges, and a dining facility. But no armories.

We exit the heavy steel door and immediately notice that the building second closest to us, the dorms for the elite Iraqi counterterrorism force Perry has spent nine years training, is half engulfed in flames. The fire trucks are on scene and are pumping water into the missing roof. We walk closer to the building, to where we see Hisham standing, supervising the fire chief, who has arrived in an inconspicuous tan Mitsubishi Pajero. The fire in the part of the building closest to us appears to have been extinguished, but in the part of the structure on the far side, flames are still jumping out of the missing roof. "Is anyone still inside?" I ask Hisham.

"*La, la, maku mushkila*," he says without facing me, and he waves and walks away to make adjustments to the rescue pumper.

An Iraqi soldier, part of a unit that works primarily at night—who has evacuated the building in his pajamas—returns with a Halligan tool, a combination of an ax and a crowbar designed for dynamic entry. Some of the U.S. Special Forces guys I work with thought it important to train me in proper dynamic entry procedures, so they took me out to their mock-up village and had me practice hooking the ax part of the tool into the door while someone else used a hammer to apply enough force to break the door open. Then I got to be the person on the hammer. Then they taught me to be the third member of the breaching team, who stood behind the Halligan holder and ran into the building first with a flashlight and my long rifle.

"Someone must still be inside," Sarah says, looking at the Halligan-wielding Iraqi. *Mushkila kirbala.*

The Iraqi in his pajamas does not have a breaching team. He has no one to hammer the flat side of his tool to drive open the door. Instead, he runs toward a window and swings the ax into it, breaking the glass so he can climb up the air conditioning unit on the ground and jump in. Sarah, Hameed, and I watch this act of heroism from the side of the rescue pumper, which continues to arc water into the building. The pajamaed Iraqi yells from inside, and two other soldiers come running to the broken-out window. From the broken window emerges a flat-screen TV. Then a DVD player. Then another TV. Then a night vision device. Finally, the pajamaed Iraqi returns to the window with his rifle and hops down onto the air conditioner. He is black with the smudges of his burned American-funded property and coughing.

By now, the entire building seems to have been extinguished. The roof is gone, and as the smoke lifts, we see the frame of the interior, charred and wilting. There are no longer beds and lockers, but piles of springs and melted plastic. The deputy brigade commander is on scene, and he enters the building, despite Hisham's fire chief telling him not to. Other soldiers are reentering the building to rescue their belongings. Not all of them made it in time to save their TVs and DVD players. Some soldiers come out of the building with melted rifles, pistols, and DVDs and lay them on the ground in front of me.

Hisham walks over to us and looks at me. Before he says anything, he touches the congealed sides of my hair, which have melted a little in the afternoon sun and in the shadow of a burning building. He moves his fat, rough, fatherly fingers over my side-swept bangs and says something to Hameed. With a dorm smoldering behind him, Hameed says something back and then interprets, "He knows why they call you *Naqueeb Jameela*."

Hisham turns and shouts instructions to the fire chief, who

45

dismisses both rescue pumpers who called someone from this unit, confirmed the fire, and responded appropriately. He paces around the perimeter of the building and shouts to the deputy brigade commander through the broken-out window. They point at the roof, at the window, at the melted U.S.-issued equipment Perry and his men gave them to execute missions. Then the deputy brigade commander waves his hands in the air, and Hisham walks back to his car and motions for Hameed, Sarah, and me to follow him. We get in his car and drive back to his office. On the way, he says, "Ali says that it looks like an electrical fire. That there was a short."

I think of the fans and the long strings of exposed copper wire running across each wall, taped into a socket. We park in front of Hisham's building and follow him in. "He wants to know how you think the response was," Hameed says. I look at Sarah, who nods.

"It was very good," I say. "Your men saved the other dorms adjacent to that building and maybe saved the lives of the men inside. Do you know how many soldiers lived in that dorm?" I ask.

Hisham opens the top drawer of his desk and takes a three-inch union joint, gives it to Sarah, and begins speaking to Hameed. Hameed points to me; then he takes out his cell phone, shakes it like a can of spray paint, and shrugs. "He wants to know why Schwab didn't go to the barber," Hameed says.

"You will need to find a place for all those men who lost their rooms," I say. Hameed repeats Hisham's question.

"Schwab didn't need a haircut yet," I say as Hameed interprets. "And I knew your barbers would do a good job, so I went."

Hisham smiles, nods. "He says he wishes all his advisers were like you. You care about his men and you try to help. If they were all like you, then they could do everything they need to and the U.S. could leave. But you are the only good one. And you are beautiful." Hameed pauses and asks Hisham something. "He says anything you need while you are here, you ask Hisham."

Hisham nods again and motions for our dismissal. Instead of shaking my hand after he dismisses us, he hugs me and again runs his fingers across my bangs. He says something to Hameed as we leave his office to walk back to our high-walled compound and toward the smoldering Iraqi dorm. Sarah passes a three-inch gray PVC union joint back and forth in her hands as we walk through the steel door. Flo is smoking a cigarette under the canopy when we get back.

"Seriously," Flo says to me, "what the fuck?"

4

The Breath of Allah

"I THOUGHT STEROIDS CAUSED SHRINKAGE," SCHWAB SAYS as he sits on the wooden bench under the canopy.

"I just don't understand why he wasn't wearing anything." I sit across from him on the horseshoe-shaped bench. "The sunburn."

"Did it look shriveled to you?" he asks.

"I didn't look," I say.

"How could you not have looked?"

Our two troops in Basrah work with a naval special warfare team—the SEALs. Unlike the Green Berets Schwab and I live and work with—who are interesting and, by and large, low key—the SEALs are crazy. Schwab has visited them more than once and tried to warn me. He goes periodically to make sure our two troops down there are still alive, and he discovered after his first visit that they were living in a truck because the SEAL team didn't exactly know where to put them. Since this discovery, he makes regular visits to ensure they haven't been evicted from the dwelling they were given, and that they still have keys to the office they work out of.

We went down to visit them together this time, hoping two of us could negotiate better conditions than one alone and, despite having been told more than once that both of us would be coming, and that I am not a man, they were utterly shocked when I got off the helicopter. The first one that saw me looked at my haircut and told me I looked like a softball coach. He took a bite of an apple and pitched it underhand, like a softball, at Schwab, who tried to catch it but watched it bounce off his torso instead. Their main bathroom is a trough that drains into an unknown destination in the sand. One of them was throwing knives at a cardboard box labeled "PLANS" as we walked by. Another one walked by us wearing a tan T-shirt and pink flip-flops. And no other clothes.

"Doesn't she look like a softball coach?" the first one asked the pantless one.

No pants winked at me and made a motion like he was swinging a softball bat—which, as it turns out, causes everything to swing. Schwab is convinced they're all on steroids.

"You had to have looked," Schwab says. "Was he your type?"

"What the fuck is wrong with you?" I ask.

"Not your type. What is?"

"Someone who wears pants," I say.

Schwab slouches on the bench, leans back, and closes his eyes. I stare at him for a minute and consider what his type might be. Though he talks about his wife, I've not yet seen a picture of her. I wonder if he also has an affinity for shorter brunettes with glasses, though Annie's hair is more a dirty blond than brunette.

I slouch back on my side of the horseshoe, close my eyes, and think of her. The last time I saw her, before I left for training in New Jersey, was in a hotel room at the Boom Town Casino in Bossier City. I had moved everything I owned into a storage unit, and my parents had flown out to take my dog and my car back to Albuquerque after they dropped me off at the airport the next day. They were staying at my house the last night before moving the bed into the storage unit. I told them it was because there was only one bed in my hotel room.

In room 312, a deluxe double queen, Annie knocked on the door and came in. By then, we didn't have much to talk about. We had spent a week together in Durango, skiing Red Mountain Pass over the holidays, and outside of skiing and sex, it had become clear there wasn't much we did well together. She was moving to Durango to run title for an oil and gas company out there and ski more, and I was moving to New Jersey and then Baghdad to do something I couldn't explain. There would be no skiing.

"I brought some ski porn," she said, took out her laptop, turned on *Blizzard of AAHHHs*, and turned out the lights. She set the computer down on one of the beds and we lay down on the other. After we watched the first few scenes, which we'd watched together a half dozen times, she slipped her hand under my shirt and kissed my neck. Her hands were warm, and her lips had the rough crackle of someone who prefers to be outside. They were one of her best features. She grabbed my third and fourth fingers on my left hand, kissed them, and winked at me. Her breathing was always calm, even as she wrestled off my clothes, piece by piece, while the flickering screen with men skiing Chamonix in onesies provided the backlight. "Me first tonight," she said, rolled onto her back, and helped me take her clothes off.

The first time we slept together, she asked me if I hummed. "No one has ever made me feel like that," she told me. I don't hum, but I take care to not do anything too quickly. She gasped, grabbed a pillow off the bed, and ran her hands through my hair. "Oh, fuck," she whispered once, then twice, and then a third time. She started to twist off to her right, driven by the rotational inertia of a force I had created. She grabbed my shoulders and pulled me closer to her. I kissed the side of her neck while she rocked slightly side to side. She took a few deep breaths, her body rigid and burning, before she fell limp onto the mattress.

Then she kissed me on the lips. Barely at first, and then for longer, and then with more intention. She ran her fingers over me, tracing my features. She kissed her way down my body. "I might hum," she said and took a deep breath. I don't think she did. She didn't have to. She was also deliberate, with a one-one-thousand-two-one-thousand-three-one-thousand kind of pace. I felt the heat building between us, focused energy starting like a small red firework in the dark, sparking kindling and then growing stronger with each breath. I twisted, driven by the intense heat, and pulled her closer as she fanned the flames. She kissed her way back up my body and lay beside me with her head resting on her hand.

We watched the movie. They were skiing Squaw. When it was over, she gathered her clothes and put them back on, letting me button her shirt. "I hope you don't die," she said, kissed me, and walked out.

"Me too," I say.

"You too, what?" Schwab asks.

I open my eyes to see him staring at me from across the bench, cleaning dirt from under his fingernails with a large spring-assisted knife. I stare at the knife for a minute.

"I pulled it out of the side of the cardboard box," he says, closes the knife, and springs it open again.

Hameed comes to sit on the horseshoe between Schwab and me.

"How was Basrah?" he asks.

"I have no fucking clue why civilization started here," Schwab says.

Hameed laughs, raising only his left shoulder. "You see," he says, "they started at the coast and began walking north. But they got too lazy to go any further, so they quit in Baghdad." He laughs some more.

Schwab sits with his mouth open and nods. "Most realistic explanation I've ever heard." He flicks the knife closed and back open.

Hameed rocks slowly back and forth on the bench. "Hisham called," he says. "There's a new unit coming to live on base and they need some things. He hopes you can help."

"What sort of things?" I ask him. Usually, when Ahmed or Fadhil say they need "things," it could be anything from black tea to a helicopter. When Hisham asks for things, it is usually propane or mattresses.

"Some beds, air conditioners, and a big water tank."

"How big of a water tank?" I ask.

Hameed shrugs and makes a circle with his arms. We have a few water tanks on this base. One is on our American compound. It is a thousand-gallon tank and is fed from the Baghdad water supply. We were told not to drink it because it has never been confirmed safe by an American bioenvironmental engineer. Some people are afraid to brush their teeth in it and instead pour bottled water over their toothbrushes every day. I have no qualms about brushing my teeth with Baghdad water, especially after eating fish caught with a grenade and cooked on a trash-can lid. Still, I don't make coffee with it.

The other water tanks belong to the Iraqis and are also fed by Baghdad water. One is near the second entry gate of the compound. Occasionally, when coming back onto the base, I see Iraqi men who have stripped down to their underwear swimming in this tank. They wave at me as I drive by. I most certainly would not brush my teeth with this water. The second Iraqi tank Hisham's men maintain. It is in the center of their dorms, and he has installed a lock on the top, to prevent swimming, and an in-line filter on the outflow. Hisham has his men sample the water every other week for pH levels and mineral content. I would probably make coffee with this water.

"When do they need this stuff?" I ask Hameed.

He shrugs again, gets up, and leaves.

"Good luck with that, Coach." Schwab closes the knife and walks away.

"THE MINIGUN," AARON EXPLAINS, "HAS SIX INDEPENDENTLY firing barrels and can fire three thousand rounds a minute." He is the weapons specialist for the team and has long promised we can cut a car in half with the mini before I leave. He hasn't found the car yet, so we're going to try to cut some large wooden structures in half instead.

"It shoots so fast rounds will cook off in the chamber due to the temperature of the metal. A lot of times," he explains, "the gun shoots so fast and is so hot not all of the powder ignites, and as the barrel cycles, it explodes the residual and shoots a flame out the front."

He is liberally applying a white gun lube to the weapon. He dips his hand in a quart-sized can of white viscous cream that looks like the kind of lard used to make real tortillas. He rubs one of the long metal barrels down with lube and looks at me. "You a lube kind of person?"

"I've never shot this before," I say.

Working the lard slowly up and down one of the barrels, he stares at me for a moment, then looks back at the weapon. "Can you lube the housing?" he asks, passing the bucket to me and pointing to the part with six cylinders where the barrels sit. I dip my third and fourth finger into the lube and begin to work it into the first of six cylinders.

"Anyway, people here call that flame that comes out the front of the mini the Breath of Allah. In Afghanistan, they call it Dragon's Breath. Either way, don't shoot this for longer than three-second bursts. That's still 150 rounds. That's plenty. If you shoot it for longer, the timing messes up and no amount of lube will fix it."

He wipes the lard off his hands and watches as I finish lubing the last two housings before he finishes assembly. So far, the .50 cal is the biggest gun I've shot. It is big and loud and lets you and everyone around you know you've shot it. If you shoot tracers out of it, it is big and loud and shoots small, intermittent red fireworks into the Iraqi night. The recoil shakes you, drives you back, and pulls toward the gun with every round. The mini, on the other hand, isn't recoil fired. It is electrically fired. Some say it offers no feedback on how you are shooting it, with or without tracers. But if you pay attention to it, and don't do anything too quickly, you can feel the slight hum of the housings and the rotational inertia trying to pull the entire assembly to the right. It is more nuanced than the .50, and far more satisfying. I aim it at the base of the hill we usually shoot things into and squeeze— one-one-thousand-two-one-thousand-three-one-thousand— and let go. "Oh, fuck," I say out loud.

The bottom of the berm has turned into a small dust storm as shells clink and pour off the roof of the gun truck the mini is mounted to. Aaron motions a vertical line with his hand and points at the wooden structure. I line up the mini for a vertical cut to be made entirely with lead projectiles. Despite it being midnight, he puts on his green sunglasses, smiles, and watches the intermittent red fireworks slowly catch the rigid structure on fire until it splits in half and falls limp to the earth.

HAMEED COMES TO GET ME AS I SIP COFFEE ON THE BENCH. "Hussein wants to talk to you. In his new office." The new office, funded, I'm told, entirely with about two million U.S. dollars, is a two-story building complete with gold windows, intricate ceiling paintings reminiscent of the Alhambra, a more fully equipped galley to make better cardamom chai, two fountains (from Baghdad water), two waterfalls (also from Baghdad water), and a jacuzzi in each of Hussein and Fadhil's private back rooms. A southwestern-style corral fence surrounds the front walkway. As Hameed and I walk around the fence to get into the building, I see what looks like a dirty rolled-up rug near the air conditioner. The kind a mob boss would roll up a dead body in for disposal. As we walk closer to the entrance, I discover that this is not, in fact, a rug concealing a dead human body. It is instead the dead body of a newly slaughtered sheep. An extremely large knife sits, soaked in blood, next to the corpse. Two of Fadhil's men hose down the front porch where, apparently, moments before its death, the sheep shat on the steps out of fright or anticipation.

Hussein gives us a tour, careful to point out the jacuzzi. I pretend to be more interested in the jade chess set sitting in front of his desk. It is frozen mid-game; the green jade queen holds the black onyx king in check, protected only by a castle. Hussein says something to Hameed, who points at me and shrugs. He pulls 90,000 dinar out of his pocket and hands it to Hameed with a piece of paper, and Hussein leads us out.

When we are on the porch again, the dead animal has been rolled over and is staring at me. The two soldiers who were cleaning the step pull up in an old jeep, drag the animal over to it, and hoist it in the back. One of them looks at me, and back at the sheep, and then back at me. He comes over and picks up the large bloody knife and looks at me again as he swings it in his hand. The trail to the jeep is a dark red stripe on the otherwise pristine steps. I stare at the empty spot previously occupied by the body of an animal slaughtered at 10:00 a.m. on a Tuesday. Hussein says goodbye to us and smooths his mustache.

"*Ma'asalama, saydie,*" I say and walk away without making eye contact.

"He wants us to go buy him some shampoo, conditioner, and Irish Spring soap. Pantene. For his daughter."

This is not the first time Hussein has asked me to buy Pantene for his daughter. Hameed told me after the first time he asked that Hussein never felt comfortable asking the men who were his advisers but that I would understand.

"Why the sheep?" I ask.

"They are celebrating the new office building. They wanted you to see it."

A FRIEND OF MINE AT THE U.S. AIR BASE NEARBY HAS A lead on a 2,500-gallon water tank. With the U.S. withdrawal from Iraq, army units are up and leaving the infrastructure they've relied on for nearly a decade. Some of them are choosing to burn their assets to the ground to prevent Iraqi use. Some are content to let them be repurposed by Iraqis or absorbed into the desert. I get some instructions on where this tank can be found, and the intel that there may be some air conditioners on the same compound, and no one would care if they went missing. In our last meeting with Hisham, Hameed arranged for his men to bring a flatbed truck on the trip, but their forklift is in the shop, so he asked if we had one. We do. It can only make left turns.

Schwab, Miller, Hameed, and I meet on the horseshoe bench under the canopy early in the morning. It would be nice if we could have put the forklift onto the flatbed, but the Iraqis have already left to do something with the truck first, so we have to drive the unidirectional forklift to the site, escorted only by our plum Trailblazer. Miller, who is usually only found when there is food or gossip to share, has volunteered to drive the forklift. We give him a map, just in case, and he climbs into the forklift's open-air cab and sets down his rifle out of the way of the controls. Schwab gets into the passenger's seat of the Trailblazer, and Hameed gets into the back seat behind me.

"Do you think we should put our flashers on?" he asks.

"Why?" I ask. He shrugs.

I turn on the radio to Hayati FM. Schwab moves to change the radio to the Armed Forces Network. I stare at him until he moves his hand away from the dial. As we leave the gate, two men in their underwear wave at us from inside the water tank.

We don't have to go far, maybe fifteen miles. But it seems like every time we have to turn, it is a right-hand turn and we have to wait for Miller to make three lefts behind us while cars honk and pass us in the oncoming traffic lanes. The machine's max speed being roughly 15 mph, it takes us more than an hour to get to the site. When we get there, the Iraqis have already moved two dozen air conditioning units from the buildings onto their flatbed, and they have gathered around the water tank and the mud bog that has formed since they drained the remaining water. Miller pulls the forklift into a small fenced-in area, the right side of his machine facing the tank. We park next to him, get out of the Trailblazer, and look at the tank. Hameed starts to talk to Hisham's men.

"They thought it would be bigger," he says.

"How big was it supposed to be?" I ask. He asks the men, who smooth their beards and mustaches, confer with one another, and say something back.

"Bigger," he says. "But they'll take it."

Miller leans out of the front of the forklift and asks how he's supposed to get a tank that size onto the flatbed. It is easily three times the size of the tiny forklift. Omar, one of Hisham's men, produces some ratchet straps from the cab of the flatbed. The six of them (who all arrived in a truck with three seats) help Omar onto the top of the tank, which has already been disconnected and wobbles freely in the mud. He lassos the top lip of the tank with a ratchet strap and throws it down, on either side, to two of the other men. They point to Miller and the forklift. Miller leans out of the cab to look at the mud, at the tank, and at the man on top of it. His rifle falls over and hits him in the back of the leg. He repositions it, wipes sweat from his forehead, and looks back at the man on top of the tank. Omar gestures inside the tank. Hameed yells, *"La, la, la!"* Miller asks us to move the car so he can make three left turns to face the tank. Positioning it on the flatbed will require a right turn. Miller wipes more sweat.

Omar insists on remaining on top of the tank while Miller tries to get the forks into the mud and underneath it. His lasso job on the opening has come off, so he is now seated, his feet dangling into the tank, holding the strap around the lip with his thighs. Miller has the tank on the forks, barely, but cannot turn any direction because of the mud. Two of Hisham's men hold the ends of Omar's ratchet strap. Two of them are pushing the forklift in the mud. Schwab, Hameed, and I stand off to the side and watch.

"None of this is a good idea," I say.

"Well," Schwab says and runs his hands through his hair, "what *has* been a good idea?"

A breeze picks up, which feels much hotter than the midmorning air. Miller has the tank on his forks, fully extended skyward, while three men push him through the mud toward the flatbed. Omar looks like a strange bull rider, bucking back and forth as the forklift lurches in the mud. By some miracle, the tank is now over the flatbed, Omar remains on top, and Miller looks like he parked the forklift under a waterfall. Once the tank is on the flatbed, Omar dismounts the tank to help attach the ratchet straps. Miller and the three mud men push the forklift out of the bog.

"Yeah, fuck this," Miller says. "I'll see you at the ranch." He makes three left turns to get out of the fenced area and starts the drive back to our compound.

"Should we wait for them?" Hameed asks and points to Hisham's men, who are learning their straps are not long enough to go around the tank and connect to the truck. We watch for a while as the men adjust the straps this way, and that way, and back this way, moving frantically in the mud.

"It's hot," Schwab says, so we get in the Trailblazer and set out to find Miller.

He hasn't made it far, though in this direction there are fewer right turns. We drive behind him, the air conditioner on blast as it approaches noon and the sun parks overhead. The mud on the forklift has dried out, forming a dark casing on most of the machine. It shudders from time to time as mud breaks free of the tracks. About five miles from our compound, the flatbed passes us. Omar is once again perched on top of the tank, feet dangling in, waving at us. Two men sit on the back of the flatbed, facing the rear. Two other men are holding the straps on the sides, leaning out over the flatbed to maintain tension. The breeze and the potholes push Omar side to side, bucking, grabbing the lip of the opening, smiling.

As Miller makes the left turn to our base, Schwab, Hameed, and I turn right to head to the U.S. air base. We're going to buy Miller a milkshake and Hussein his shampoo. The BX doesn't take dinar, so I pay with my own money while Schwab gets Miller and the rest of us large vanilla bean Frappuccinos. Hameed periodically shops for T-shirts and hats but never buys anything. Almost every time we come with him, people demand to see his credentials. Once, someone yelled at him to go back to where he came from. Which, assuming the angry man thought Hameed was Iraqi, would be right here. Instead, Hameed told me he'd be going back to California at the start of the year when his contract is up.

Back at our compound, Hameed, Schwab, Miller, and I sit under the canopy and drink our mostly melted Frappuccinos. Miller has changed his shirt, but he is still sweating excessively. He asks us what else we bought him and points to the bag sitting next to Hameed.

"Pantene Pro V," Hameed says and laughs. Miller's shiny Black head is entirely hairless. "Maybe we go see Hussein tonight?"

Hameed asks. I agree. We sit in silence for a while drinking fake vanilla bean milkshakes in the Iraqi heat.

AT 10:00 P.M. HAMEED AND I GET BACK IN THE TRAIL-blazer and head toward the new palace-office. This time of day we drive with the windows down and the AC still on. Passing the test pit, I hear the hum of the mini and see the Breath of Allah coming out the end of the barrel during a test fire for one of Aaron's team's missions. When we arrive and park in front of the corral, Hameed follows me to Hussein's office. The chessboard has not moved. Hussein shakes my hand, pulls me close for a hug, and holds on for a noticeably long time. Hameed hands him the shampoo. He says something to Hameed and takes out a picture of a short brunette with glasses.

"This is his daughter," Hameed says. "Look at how nice her hair is because of you."

I smile at Hussein. He says something to Hameed. Hameed shouts something back at him. Hussein says something else, something that takes a long time to explain. He stands up, shakes Hussein's hand, and watches as Hussein shakes my hand and holds on too long.

"Did you know the new unit coming in had working dogs?" Hameed said.

"No one mentioned it to me. Do they need anything?" I ask.

"No," Hameed said. "They died today. They were being kept in a shipping container and the air conditioners went out. It got so hot in there, they baked."

The real Breath of Allah.

5

Breechblock

IN THE MORNING, AROUND 10:00 A.M., YOU CAN FIND HASAN, the chef, at one of the kebob restaurants, hosing down his kitchen. His cooking area is a rectangle with an opening at one corner. The floor is a twenty-foot patch of concrete poured directly over the moderately leveled ground. His rectangle sits unevenly on this patch; on one side is the clear plastic case that holds the onions, bell peppers, tomatoes, cucumbers, and lemons. Opposite the vegetable case is a four-foot-long cooking surface, holding a row of charcoals, complete with a hair dryer, affixed to the end by a plentiful amount of yellow duct tape, circulating the air over it. Adjacent to the coals is the counter where our chef, dressed in an ankle-length gray robe and Adidas flip-flops, chops parsley and other herbs before he chops the freshly cut lamb. Then he forms the kebobs into one-inch-wide, six-inch-long rectangles by hand. Behind him is the counter where he assembles plates of food for his guests.

He rinses the counters and concrete slab they are built on with a garden hose connected to the Baghdad water supply. The U.S. bioenvironmental engineers that surveyed this supply six years ago reported that it was unsafe for us to drink. But outside the pallets of bottled water sitting in diminishing piles within the concrete walls of our compound, and the million-dollar Reverse Osmosis Water Purification Unit that we bought for these Iraqis, who refuse to use it, Baghdad water is all we have. So we use it, just as the Iraqis do, to bathe and supply our single functional washing machine.

After Hasan finishes with the hose, he will take a broom-shaped squeegee and pull the water off the concrete into the grass. I know about the late-morning cleaning because behind this kebob stand is a large open area the Iraqis are converting into a demonstration platform. It will host an upcoming show of force, to be performed for the benefit of Iraqi and U.S. generals, in an effort to reaffirm the Iraqis' ability to conduct operations without U.S. support. The support battalion, for which I am the only U.S. adviser, is responsible for creating the platform, providing a seating area, and clearing a secondary trash pile that has built up behind the kebob place.

Tonight Hameed and I have come to see the progress of the viewing platform and meet with Hazbar. He is the chief of logistics for the support battalion and the man who usually assumes command when Adel, the battalion commander, is absent. He has two eight-foot-high bookcases full of inventories and other papers and is the only Iraqi I have met who enjoys paperwork. His uniform is slightly different from the rest of his unit because he prefers to wear a three-inch web belt all the time and needs pants with three-inch belt loops. He is also the only Iraqi I have seen with this uniform variation, which I am told they do not purchase from the U.S. supplier that makes the rest of their uniforms. They buy it from a Pakistani company for significantly less money, along with considerably discounted counterfeit engines, car batteries, and M4 carbine parts that have interesting, frequently explosive, methods of failure.

We approach the platform from our compound to the west, passing the soldier dorms and the operations center, where late at night, over rounds of chai, these Iraqis plan missions to extract people from their homes at gunpoint. Just north of the platform is the kebob restaurant and its small patch of concrete and grass where a few sheep and chickens roam. East of the kebob place is the mud village where the Iraqis practice their tactics, where I was taught the various uses of the Halligan tool, and where the demonstration will show off Iraqi competence. The U.S. soldiers

I work with once asked me to participate in one of their training missions. I was to be a resident of this village during a raid, where they are forced to make decisions to shoot, apprehend, or ignore various residents. "Do you shoot blanks in the mud village?" I asked before I committed to being a training aid.

"No," Brandon, one of the Green Berets, told me. "We fire live. It seems stupid to send blanks to a war."

I declined the invitation.

Under the glow of portable gas-powered stadium lights, I stand with Hazbar on top of the dirt pile that forms the viewing platform. He points to the concrete blast walls that form the perimeter of the viewing platform, which they are filling with dirt. He points out how well his men can operate the crane. Then he stops as he points out that the crane, which belongs to Hisham's garrison support unit, not his support battalion, is present at all—an uncommon display of cooperation, which suggests that perhaps the Iraqis are more ready for a U.S. departure than we thought. We don't need a show of force to conclude that, just a crane and cooperative Iraqis. I nod as Hameed and Hazbar carry on a conversation. Hameed doesn't bother taking his notebook out of his back pocket for this conversation, so whatever they are discussing is between the two of them. As the cement trucks begin to arrive, Hazbar suggests that we should get out of the construction area and go have something to drink. He walks us over to the kebob restaurant, buzzing with off-duty Iraqi commandos who drive their U.S.-purchased gun trucks around the base like taxis.

Sarkis—before he left, or was removed for possibly helping purchase and traffic cocaine for the hookah boy who used to sell hookah out of the tent attached to the kebob place—told me that it was rude to not accept food and chai when offered. He taught me how to order both: *Nafra kebob, nos nos sam sumac. Chai, shukar hafif.* The first expression gets me four rectangular kebobs with sumac, a purple, lemony spice I ate here for the first time. I asked him to teach me how to say "please" as well. "You don't need to say 'please' here. You're American," he told me. When I insisted, he taught me to add *lau samahed* to the end of my requests, which Hameed later told me loosely means "if it doesn't trouble you."

Hasan asks me if I would like anything to eat or drink. *Lau samahed, nafra kebob, nos nos sam sumac. Chai, shukar hafif.* I am never sure if I should add the caveat to the end or the beginning, so I try to vary it.

Hasan leaves and returns with my kebobs and an extra-large plate of vegetables. He sits down and waves his hand at some of the commandos, who want him to leave our table so they can order from him. He points to me and says something to them, which causes these commandos to bring chairs to our table and sit down with us. "They want to know if you'll be at the demonstration," Hameed tells me.

"I'm not sure I'm invited," I tell them, and Hameed interprets.

The platform is relatively small, capable of holding about eighty people in neatly arranged rows of chairs. But, as Hazbar pointed out—before the cement trucks arrived—it will not hold that many because the space that would accommodate the first two rows will be occupied by the VIP areas: gold couches with red velvet canopies and gold-embossed tables that Adel will bring out of his office, quiet misting fans (the demonstration is at 10:00 a.m. to accommodate the U.S. and Iraqi generals, even though all the missions here are at night), and a small refrigerator full of water and a sparkling orange-flavored drink the commander of the Iraqi Special Warfare School prefers. The refrigerator is plugged into an extension cord that is plugged into an extension cord, plugged into three more extension cords, spanning roughly a quarter mile before plugging into the only power outlet at the kebob restaurant, the closest power source. The hair dryer will not be operational during the demonstration so the general's orange drinks can remain chilled.

"He says you have to come," Hameed interprets for a young-looking Iraqi wearing capri track pants with "Special Forces," in English, in gold letters down the side and a tan tank top with irregularly sized black horizontal stripes.

I nod and eat my kebobs while Hasan and Hameed argue over

something and frequently point at the chicken perched on top of the fridge that holds Coke in eight-ounce glass bottles, the sparkling orange-flavored drink, and liquid yogurt in what look like the Iraqi version of Yahoo bottles.

When I try to pay, Hasan shakes his head and waves his arms. Ever since I helped him get a toaster and a TV onto the base, through U.S.-controlled territory, he has not let me pay for food. And ever since I helped Hazbar, who owns the kebob place, acquire a few dozen air conditioners and twenty-three beds in various stages of U.S. abandonment, I have been invited to dinner every night I see him. I try to limit dinner here to once a week; any more than that seems greedy. I say thank you and shake hands with Hasan, who points at his TV with gratitude. As Hameed and I leave, we almost get run over by a group of commandos driving their gun truck. In the rearview mirror, I see Hasan and Hazbar walk over to the driver, pull him out of the seat by the collar of his FC Barcelona jersey, point at the TV and back at our car, and yell as only Iraqis can.

The next morning, after the near miss with the reckless up-armored taxi service, we go to meet Hazbar and check the progress of the concrete pour. In Adel's office, before we leave for the platform, he brings out his diagram and explains the seating arrangement to me. Blue ceramic tiles will line the sides of the stairs leading up to the platform, and the commandos will use the area labeled "sand table" to present their mission briefing to the generals on the gold couches. Hameed scribbles notes in his green notebook with a semi-functional U.S. government–issued pen and suggests that we should go see the platform.

We get into Adel's gold Mitsubishi and leave his office, and we drive behind the kebob restaurant and to the platform—which, overnight, has gone from a collection of short concrete blast walls to an actual platform, now hardening in the Iraqi midmorning sun. A mason sits on the steps and begins to inlay blue ceramic tiles into the sides of the stairway. Adel parks the car, and we dismount to make a complete lap around the platform. We start at the west stairs. These are for the average viewers, so they will not get the blue accent tiles. Neither will the steps be properly leveled or evenly spaced. The platform slab is still curing, so we walk around the back to see some of Adel's men painting the rear of the platform fuchsia, yellow, and lime green, the colors of their unit. As we walk around to the front, some other men are painting the unit patch on the blast walls near the stairs. Someone is painting the Iraqi flag next to someone painting over what Hameed tells me are Saddam's initials. They had been spray-painted onto the blast wall next to the "77" imprint they all bear. Apparently it is the mark of the company that mass produced concrete blast walls, in Kurdish Arbil, in four-, twelve-, and twenty-foot-high options, following the U.S. invasion—an operation that made 77's net worth jump from approximately $400,000 in 2003 to $300 million just five years later.

There are millions of these walls here, and as U.S. forces withdraw, they are being increasingly repurposed. Last week, we noted houses made entirely out of these blast walls. The only additions to each house were a roof and some form of door. Some of the walls of these houses still displayed murals, or half murals, from the American units that had required twelve feet of one-foot-thick concrete security for the past eight years. One house was a combination of the walls from a former Combat Support Hospital (CSH painted with half the red cross on one wall), the walls from the Fourth Brigade Combat Team in 2008, rearranged out of order, and a blue tarp ceiling held in place by plywood and large pots on the roof.

As one of Adel's men paints over Saddam's initials on the U.S. barrier, which is now as common to this country's landscape as date palms, Hazbar points out where they have cemented an extension cord into the platform so it is not a tripping hazard. It runs out the side near the uneven, unlevel stairs and is buried in a shallow trench on the other side of what is now the platform's dirt parking lot. The orange cord jumps out of the ground again like an Iraqi Loch Ness monster and weaves its way to the kebob restaurant, where we can see Hasan beginning to clean his patch of concrete. Hazbar motions us toward the restaurant, and we shake hands with Adel, who is leaving today for a vacation with his wife. Adel drives away as we walk to the shaded part of Hasan's grass.

We wave to Hasan as he gets the squeegee out and shoos the chicken back to the top of the fridge. We sit down at one of the white plastic tables, and Hazbar offers Hameed and me liquid yogurt. I decline the yogurt. Hazbar offers me some water from Hasan's washing hose. I decline, so he returns with a Coke in an eight-ounce glass bottle. This is the first full Coke I have ever had, and I later discover why some people suggest that it can clean corrosion off car batteries, Pakistani or otherwise. We sip our beverages while a sheep naps under the canopy by the rectangular concrete kitchen and the chicken tries to adjust itself on top of the refrigerator that keeps Coke and drinkable yogurt.

Hasan comes to join our table. He is Hazbar's brother and now lives on this Iraqi base with Hazbar and his family because of the repeated death threats he received in Diyala, where their family is originally from. Hazbar has a date farm there that he has not surrendered, and he makes periodic trips, when on leave from his unit, to monitor its operation—despite the danger such hands-on management poses.

Hameed takes out his notebook and begins to take notes. Hasan explains that, due to the demonstration's construction, Hasan's house behind the kebob restaurant must be bulldozed to allow an unobstructed view from the viewing platform when the primary ground assault force enters the mud village. "He wonders if there is anything you can do to help," Hameed says. Hasan looks at me and points at his house, small and built out of brown mud, with a small garden, under a canopy, that produces some of the vegetables we eat, after dark, at this restaurant. A sheep is asleep in his front yard, and clothes hang on a line out front like prayer flags made of gray robes.

"Who decided that his house needed to be torn down?" I ask Hazbar.

He shrugs, says something that Hasan interrupts, and points to the brigade headquarters. "General Hussein," Hameed interprets for me.

Hussein is much taller than Hazbar, has killed a lot of people and, when not asking for shampoo, tells me so. A scar spans the length of the left side of his face, disappearing briefly into his mustache and tapering off just above his jawline. He holds on the longest of all the Iraqis I meet with when we shake hands, whispers things into my ear in Arabic, and gives Hameed stacks of money to buy him Irish Spring soap and Pantene conditioner for his daughter. He is the deputy in charge of the brigade and still leads his men on missions. Sarkis told me that he was in the Republican Guard and still waits on Saddam's return to power, despite Saddam having been hanged more than half a decade ago.

I try to avoid meeting with Hussein because his embraces, once noticeably long, are now uncomfortably long, and because he is the kind of man who would unilaterally decide to bulldoze someone's house to prevent a convoy from being obstructed for a few seconds during a two-hour demonstration. But I also know that of anyone on this entire base, I have the best chance of talking him into keeping Hasan's house upright because of my blond American hair and my gifts of soap.

I tell Hazbar and Hasan I will talk to Hussein later in the day. Hasan claps his hands and grabs my hand in gratitude. Hazbar offers me another Coke, which I decline, and we all walk back to the support battalion headquarters, where we left our car. Hameed tells me Hazbar will do some paperwork for a few hours to cool off before he goes back out to the platform. I agree with his plan, shake his hand, and leave.

Hameed finds my meetings with Hussein comical. Sarkis, before he left to evade indictment, used to time how long Hussein shook my hand and hugged me. The longest time was forty-seven seconds. Hameed has continued this ritual and is hopeful

I will break a minute before I leave Iraq. Fifty-seven seconds is the current record. I ask Hameed to call Hussein and schedule a meeting to discuss the logistics of the demonstration. He tells us to come over to his office immediately, so we leave directly from the support battalion building to the headquarters. When we arrive, we walk in and meet one of the only three women who work for this unit. Two of them are secretaries and have also been arbitrarily assigned other jobs, within their units, that their male bosses found too insignificant for men to do. This mostly involves upkeep of various inventories and records. The third woman is sleeping with Ahmed, the brigade director of logistics. She has no noticeable job to perform, so she sits all day in the logistics office and adjusts her sky-blue eye makeup and calls for more chai without ever talking to me.

The woman we meet at Hussein's office is older than Hussein, and at one point in her life she had acid thrown on her face by someone from Saddam's regime because of something her uncle allegedly said to a policeman. In exchange for English lessons, which I am terrible at providing, Mara has taught me how to wrap my head in one of the scarves Hussein gave me when I first arrived. She was assigned the task of managing the brigade's ammunition supply, so I have taught her how to count to five million and identify different types of bullets by their nomenclature—5.56 ball; 7.62 link (for U.S. weapons); 7.63x39mm (for Kalashnikovs); det cord; AN-M14 incendiary grenade, firing adapter. I ask Hameed to ask her if she would like to learn anything else, and she says no, just the types of bullets.

She greets us in the hall and points at my head. It upsets her that I do not normally cover my head, so she has taken to having a few scarves on standby for days I arrive without one, which is every day. My recent haircut seems to have caused extra alarm. She presents me with a purple scarf and evaluates how I wear it. She offers a suggestion on my use of the across-the-shoulder wrap and points to the word for "green smoke," one of various types of grenades in our inventory. After I say it enough times, she writes down the phonetic pronunciation in Arabic and walks us into Hussein's office. Hameed readies his watch.

Twenty-eight seconds today. Hussein must be busy. The woman chuckles when Hameed says "twenty-eight," and she walks back to her table with books and binders of numbers and ammunition names. Hussein calls for chai. Hameed explains the issue with bulldozing Hasan's house. Hussein shakes his head and yells his words at Hameed. "He says it blocks the view. The prime minister might come to this. We can't block the prime minister's view," Hameed interprets.

"Is there somewhere else here Hasan can live with his sheep and chickens?" I ask.

Hussein shakes his head. He strokes his mustache and speaks, and Hameed interprets, "He says they need blank ammunition for the demonstration. They can't fire live. Do you have any blank ammunition?"

Mara walks in from the hall, smiles at me, and says, "Blank."

Hussein yells at her and points to the door. She, unlike the other two women who work here, is not afraid to respond. She says something back before she turns to me, smiles again, and leaves.

"If we find him blanks, will he not bulldoze Hasan's house?" I ask and Hameed interprets.

Hussein shrugs and strokes his mustache. He looks at a different ivory and obsidian chess set that sits on a coffee table in front of his desk. The obsidian queen has had the ivory king in checkmate the entire time I've been in this country, and like the other chess sets, the pieces haven't moved. "*Na'am*," he says and waves his hands for us to leave. We stand, shake hands (eighteen seconds), and Hameed shuts the door behind him as we walk out.

We stop in front of Mara's desk. She has taken a binder off the shelf and turned the yellow pages until she found one where she wrote the Arabic phonetic equivalent next to the word "blank."

"Do you have these?" I ask her. Hameed interprets.

She adjusts my scarf and says, "*Na'am*, sixty thousand."

"Can I see them?" I ask her.

She nods and we walk out of the headquarters hallway, down the street, to the First Battalion's armory. Mara takes out a set of keys, opens the door, and shows us in. Inside the armory are neatly arranged rows of body armor, M4 carbines, pistols, helmets, and night vision devices for the battalion's six hundred soldiers. Behind the gear racks is an area for their crew-served weapons, .50 cals, 240Bs, 249s, all U.S., and behind that, a separate area for ammunition. Every day I meet with Ahmed, the brigade director of logistics, he asks for more ammo. They don't have enough to do missions, he says. At this suggestion, Mara, from the hallway, makes noises that cause Ahmed's blue-painted girlfriend to abandon her makeup adjustments and go speak to Mara. I can see now that Mara's noises are an expression of disagreement. In front of me, neatly stacked, are roughly one and a half million rounds of ammunition. "She counted them all herself," Hameed interprets.

Mara points to all different types of ammo and motions me to a corner with three thousand twenty-round boxes of 5.56 blanks. I pick one up, open it, and verify the ammo. Its crimped top edge and NATO stamp confirm that, indeed, at some point in the eight years of this war, this Iraqi battalion acquired roughly $20,000 worth of ammunition that won't kill anyone. "They'll need about five thousand rounds for the demo and practices," I say and Hameed interprets to Mara. She takes out a notepad and writes notes.

"Two hundred fifty box," she says.

I nod. "We also need blank firing adapters," I tell Hameed, who interprets this.

"Fire adapter," Mara says and walks us to another part of the armory. In a loose pile on the floor are hundreds of the yellow M4 BFAS, still in their plastic wrap, contained in this space by a perimeter of ammo cans. A blank firing adapter is comprised of a cubelike housing for a screw plug that gets inserted into the end of the barrel and tightened into place. Ones for the M16 are red. BFAS for the M4 are yellow. They prevent the gas from the blank round from escaping the barrel, which would normally be sealed by the projectile of a live round. The gas pressure caused by the BFA pushes the breechblock of the weapon back where it would be if a regular bullet were fired, cycling a new round into the chamber. The drawbacks of BFAs: Because less gas than normal escapes the plugged barrel, weapons with BFAs build up carbon very rapidly and need frequent cleaning; the screws that hold the yellow ones in place are not very good (despite costing about $14 each) and fall out during routine training; if a regular round is fired with a BFA, it will destroy the weapon and has, in a few cases, been known to explosively exit the weapon out of the side, killing the shooter.

"Six hundred eighty-one," Mara says, pointing to the pile.

"So we don't have to do anything, then," Hameed says to me and puts his notepad back into his pocket.

I shake my head. Hussein won't use these if he believes he already had them. If I have learned anything here, it is that the Iraqis value having an asset over actually using it for its intended purpose, even when that intended purpose has no lethal consequence to operations in a war. If Hussein knows he has these already, he will find a way to move them elsewhere, claim I overheated and hallucinated the bullets, yell at Mara, and request more, usually in ten times the quantity he actually needs. I know this because he has done it before with .50 cal rounds, tan underwear sets like his commandos wear to the kebob place, and night vision helmet mounts—all items he has plenty of, but refuses to issue to his soldiers.

"Mara, can we put one hundred of the firing adapters and two hundred fifty boxes of blanks aside, somewhere near the front?" I ask and Hameed interprets, drawing his notepad again.

Mara nods, and we begin to relocate the boxes and BFAs. After ten minutes of moving blank bullets—and the muzzle plugs that make rifles cycle—to another part of the armory, we walk her back to her desk in the hallway across from Hussein's office. I hug her, give back the scarf so it is ready for me next time, and invite her to dinner at the kebob restaurant tonight. She declines, and she kisses my cheeks and runs her hands through my hair before we leave her to practice the new words I gave her today: M203 grenade launcher, sniper night sight.

On the way back to our compound, I ask Hameed to call Hussein in three or four hours and tell him that we put some blanks and firing adapters near the front of the First Battalion armory for the demonstration. Three or four hours later, while I am sitting at my desk watching sand blow across the sunbaked mud underneath the trailer, through the hole in the floor, Hameed comes in and tells me that we have to go eat kebobs tonight.

"Can we bring anything?" I ask, still feeling like the dinner guest that never contributes to the meal.

"*Hubbuz*, maybe," Hameed says, and a few hours later, when it's dinnertime and the sun has long been down in Iraq, we get in the car and drive to the bakery, where I order *ashra hubbuz, lau samahed* and hand the baker two U.S. dollars in exchange for ten pieces of freshly fired flatbread. He waves his hands when I give him the money, so I leave it on the counter and smile on my way out.

Hubbuz in hand, we drive to the kebob place, dodging gun truck taxis and energetic Iraqi commandos preparing for tonight's missions. Hussein, Hazbar, Ahmed, and the blue eye makeup lady are already sitting around a table, laughing and drinking chai, when we park and get out of our car. Hussein and Hazbar wave to us. Ahmed pulls a machine gun from underneath the table, points it at the chicken on top of the fridge, then pulls the bolt back to the rear and locks it in place before setting the gun on his lap. We walk up to their table with our offering and see they have already ordered kebobs and vegetables and were waiting on us to arrive. Hussein stands up, grabs my hand, leans in. Hameed and Hazbar, who has caught on to the ritual, look at their watches while Hussein whispers things in Arabic into my ear. I try to remember them so Hameed can interpret them later, but I figure there is an equal chance of them being sweet words of love and adoration and a gentle way to say, "I would kill you and the rest of the Americans if given the chance." After fifty-three seconds, Hussein lets go and I shake Hazbar's and Ahmed's hands. I go to kiss blue eye makeup's cheeks, but she pretends to not notice me and looks across the grass at a group of commandos smoking non-cocaine-laced hookah.

Ahmed takes the M4 off his lap and passes it to me across the table. Hazbar is assembling his kebobs with the fresh *hubbuz* and charred tomatoes. In front of Hazbar is a plate of fresh peaches he brings in for me from his farm in Diyala. He smiles at me as he squeezes the lemon basras, a lime boiled in salt and sundried, on the meat. Hussein sits down and says, "Ahmed brought this brand-new M4 for you. It still has the U.S.-issue tag on it."

I look at the weapon, first making sure the chamber is clear and the weapon is safe, and notice that it is the first brand-new M4 I have ever seen, indeed complete with a U.S.-issue tag. Ahmed reaches into his pocket and takes out a magazine, which he passes me across the plate of onions, bell peppers, banana peppers, and tomatoes. Hasan brings everyone a round of chai, *shukar hafif*, and sits in the empty chair next to his brother. Hussein says, "If you fire the entire magazine of blanks and it all works, Hasan will keep his house." Then Hussein strokes his mustache, assembles a kebob, and begins eating it while Ahmed passes a blank firing adapter across the table.

I screw in the BFA as tight as I can get it. I can see only the first two rounds in the magazine, so they are the only two I know for certain have the crimped tops, confirming they are blank rounds with no projectile to send down the barrel into the BFA, and no other components that would explosively and lethally depart the weapon. I want to empty the magazine entirely and check each round, so I begin to remove the bullets. "*La, la, la!*" Hussein yells at me. Hameed interprets, "He says you can't do that. Don't you trust them to have loaded the magazine properly?"

No. I do not. But with four Iraqi men staring at me, and one woman who refuses to acknowledge my existence, I begin to put the four bullets I have removed back into the magazine. Behind us, FC Barcelona has been awarded a penalty on the television and the commandos around the hookah set down their pipes to watch the result. I have seen six of the thirty rounds in the magazine, so I know at least the first six trigger squeezes won't kill or badly maim me. The rest won't either, *insha'allah*. Hasan gets up to bring me more chai. Hussein strokes his mustache and eats with his mouth open. Hazbar eats around the pit of a peach that drips juice down his arm. Hameed moves his chair closer to Hussein's, widening the space between his seat and mine. Ahmed strokes the leg of blue eye makeup, who is eyeing the group of commandos.

I insert the magazine into the magazine well and send the bolt forward. I am not entirely sure where to point the gun to shoot off thirty blanks around a plastic dinner table, so I try to point it up, over everyone's heads, and away from the houses and dorms. I aim it in the direction of the demonstration platform, which is dark, painted, and still curing. Ahmed leans over the table. Hussein leans back in his chair. Hazbar sets the peach pit down. David Villa converts the penalty.

I switch the selector to auto and squeeze the trigger. The weapon cycles. I squeeze again. It cycles again. And again. And again, and again, and again. Six rounds in, Hameed interprets as Hussein says, "Put it on burst."

I move the lever to burst and prepare to fire the remaining twenty-four unverified rounds three at a time. Hameed moves closer to Hussein and plugs his ears. Ahmed and Hazbar have also put their index fingers into their ear canals. Blue eye makeup gets up from the table and joins the commandos, who are watching me empty an M4 magazine around a table of kebobs. The chicken adjusts herself on the fridge.

I squeeze the trigger again. Hazbar flinches each time a round fires its projectile-free gas burst down the barrel into the end of the BFA. In eight trigger squeezes, the bolt locks to the rear. I safe the weapon, drop the magazine, and clear the chamber before handing the hot, smoking M4 back to Ahmed, who sets it on the table in front of him, stands, collects blue eye makeup, and leaves. Hussein says something that Hameed does not interpret for me, says something to Hasan, rises, shakes my hand, whispers into my ear, takes the weapon, and also departs. Hasan returns to the table with fresh chai for us, sets it down, and hugs me while he says, "*Shukran, Jameela, shukran. Shukran jazeera!*"

Hazbar passes me a peach, and we move our chairs to watch the TV.

6

Repetitive and Unnecessary

"WE CAN ONLY PLUG ONE THING IN OVER HERE," MATT SAYS as I wipe the fine desert sand off one of the treadmills. "If we have more than one thing going, it blows the power to the whole compound. Sometimes it catches stuff on fire."

He points to a stationary bike thrown behind the treadmills, one pedal melted totally off and the seat drooping to the side, the metal seat post slanted like it still oozes through the plastic.

Matt, the adviser for the Iraqi special warfare school, brought me to the gym when I told him I am going to run a marathon when I get back to the States in three or four months. We used to count our time left by how many more times we'd need to wash our clothes in the semi-functional washer, but after it went from 10 to 13 to some number after 15, because of some logistical problems with our replacements, we stopped using that metric. The moving deadline has caused some issues with my training program, but I decided running extra is better than running not enough. Matt told me running a marathon sounded repetitive and useless; even so, he brought me over to the other side of our compound and led me into the tent that is partitioned into two parts, one half a gym, one half the vehicle repair tent. Everything smells like melting rubber and diesel. The gym side has a separate little room in the back, evidently supposed to be an office area, and on the vehicle maintenance side, it is. But here, there are just three treadmills in boxes collecting dust.

We walk into the main area and wait a while for our eyes to adjust to the dim blue light. Of the twelve lights on this side of the tent, which hang from the ceiling like overturned timpani drums, only three of them work. They beam a faint blue glow, which makes the climbing rope hanging from the roof support look orange. There's a rack of kettlebells near the door. There's a spin bike facing the climbing rope. There're a few medicine balls. There's a treadmill in the corner flanked by one tan fabric wall, facing another wall that is so close you can touch both walls at the same time while running. There's a barbell set and bumper plates with THOMPSON written on them in Sharpie. I don't know if Thompson is here with me now, or was here before and left his weights in this tent to wait for his return. I don't know anyone's last name on the Green Beret teams I'm with. I used to know the sergeant major's last name, but Matt, who isn't part of Perry's guys, just calls him Sergeant Major Fuckface, and now I can't remember his real name.

By the time I can see, Matt is halfway up the rope and isn't using his legs. He slides down and dusts himself off. "Fuckface probably doesn't want a lot of you air force people over here, so don't mention this to anyone else," Matt says as we walk across the floor mats toward the other door. "Actually, fuck it. Bring everyone."

Between the black rubber rectangles on the floor are small ravines of fine sand. A medium-sized camel spider, about as big as one of the 2.5-pound weights, runs in front of us and Matt kicks it into the tan fabric of the tent on the way out. He opens the door and points to the concrete blast walls, close enough to the side of the tent that the fabric smacks against them in windstorms. On the other side of those walls are the four thousand Iraqis we live with.

WITH MORE THAN HALF OF MY TEAM'S TIME HERE GONE, our air force leadership decides it's time to visit us from their headquarters in Kuwait. I meet my commander by the cars outside the blast walls that separate us from the Iraqis on this compound. He gets out and asks where my hat is. I point to the sign near our door that says "BY ORDER OF CDR NO HAT NO SALUTE AREA," enter the door access code (which is the same as the lock's default passcode, as are all the locks I've encountered here), and let them in.

We are standing under the canopy when the generator fails, and he asks for a cold bottle of water and tells me he knows we've not received most of the policies that have come down because we don't have the right internet. One of the two special agents that go with him everywhere and make sure he doesn't get assassinated walks into my office trailer to look for water. My air force boss hands me a list of the new ground travel policies and smiles as his assistant emerges with three bottles, takes two for himself, and gives the boss one. My office has the only functional fridge on our side of the compound, and it is only large enough to keep six bottles cool. It takes twenty-two hours to cool off new ones we put into it.

My commander says he was surprised to learn that my team had been reorganized by the army and sent to six different places across the country. He says he wishes he knew about it five months ago, when it happened. He says it must be hard for me to keep track of all thirty-one people on my team. He says it is hot. He says we do vital work for the U.S. Air Force and that we make him proud. Then he shakes the hands of the other six people here with me and walks to the large steel door to our compound while his assistants check under his Level VI up-armored vehicle for bombs. They almost didn't come because we told them you can't park vehicles inside the compound walls and they'd be sharing a parking lot with an Iraqi unit. He walks through the door and stands next to the sign and waits for me to salute him. I give him a thumbs-up, close the door behind him, and read the items on the list, conveniently formatted into five bullet points. He has highlighted three, four, and five.

#1: All ground movement outside of U.S.-controlled territory must have a Level III CONOP on file before departure (email is acceptable)

#2: No personnel will travel alone outside U.S.-controlled territory

#3: Women will not drive vehicles outside U.S.-controlled territory

#4: Women will not depart U.S.-controlled territory without a male service member escorting them

#5: All personnel will be properly armed outside U.S.-controlled territory

I SIT IN MY OFFICE AND SIP HOT BOTTLED WATER FROM the unlabeled bottles covered in sand. A palm tree is stamped into the white plastic cap of all of them. It's Thursday, which means it's a long run day, twenty miles. I have to plan ahead for long days because I have only one bra left that I can run in for a few hours without being chafed raw. No amount of Body Glide seems to help. For a while we had some Iraqis do our laundry for us for $2 a bag. But after the third time we sent it out, I was down four pairs of underwear and six bras. I went back to using the only washing machine here that occasionally works. Soaking clothes in warm water and Tide is better than losing all my underwear to unknown Iraqi men.

I have to run twenty miles three times before we should be going home. Today is the first. I don't usually go to the other side of the compound with its diesel-smelling, blue-glowing prison gym. Instead, I hop in my Trailblazer and drive myself to the air base not far away and use their gym and dining hall. The dining hall serves steak and lobster on Monday nights, and on Thursdays serves the best naan I've ever had. Now, with the new rules, I don't have much choice anyway.

The treadmills here shut off after ninety minutes. Once they shut off, you have to wait a few minutes for it to reset before you can turn it back on, and then you have to wait for it to go from 0 to my normal running speed of 7.3, a process that takes two minutes and seventeen seconds and all my patience to endure. My motivation for long runs is to finish before the treadmill shuts off a second time. Two restarts seem unbearable.

Even though it is the hottest part of the day, I usually run at 3:00 p.m., so I can have dinner right afterward and get ready for the 7:00 p.m. meeting with Perry and his guys. At 3:15 I tell Beck that I'm going to the gym. We share the third of this forty-foot shipping container that is our office. His side has a much larger hole in the floor than my side does, but he's closer to the AC. He nods and does what he usually does at 3:00 p.m.: takes out an Applied Aerospace Management textbook and studies for his MBA.

I run eight miles on the treadmill in the corner, staring at the side of a tan tent, before I realize my iPod has been on repeat. I've just listened to a song called "Get Around This" for more than an hour, and if the looming threat of the treadmill shutdown hadn't zapped me out of its rhythmic trance, I might have run the whole twenty miles this way. It's a catchy song with a good beat that exactly mirrors the cadence of my legs as they hop on the spinning belt of frayed gray plastic fabric.

There are three beeps before the treadmill stops. All the numbers turn to eight and flash. I straddle the sides of the slowing belt and wait for the shutdown to finish and the flashing eights to go out. I punch the "start" button until it beeps three more times and the belt starts to move. I jab my finger into the up arrow and wait for it to go from 2.0 to 7.3; then I walk on the belt until it catches up with the number and push "skip" on my iPod to get a new song.

With eleven minutes to spare, I finish the twenty miles and move the treadmill to 3.5 to walk for a bit. I bend down to pick up my water bottle from the ground. I can't keep it in the water bottle holder because that's where I keep my pistol, so I set it down beside the treadmill next to the tent wall.

When I stand back up, Matt flops his hands onto the side rail and says, "Jesus, how long were you on that thing?"

I take out my earphones. "Twenty miles," I say.

"Fuck," he says. "Hey, I need your help with some stuff. Find me after the meeting."

He checks the safety on my pistol and looks at the timer. 83:17. 83:18. 83:19. "Fuck," he says and walks toward the back door. "That seems so repetitive, shitty, and unnecessary."

A LINE OF IRAQIS WALKS PAST ME HOLDING ROCKS THE SIZE of shoe boxes. I am sitting outside under a date palm, on a flaking white plastic bench, drinking tea with Hisham. We watch the men walk by alternately lifting the rocks over their heads, yelling something in Arabic, and moving them back down against their chests, arms crossed like they are holding a flag about to be presented to the spouse of a deceased soldier. An Iraqi in a different uniform walks next to them and yells instructions. He adjusts the thick black web belt that holds his pistol. Periodically, the instructor reaches for his pistol, draws it a few inches out of the holster, and puts it back before he moves close to one of the men holding rocks to yell and point at the road.

"They keep coming," Hisham says to Hameed, who says it to me. He looks at the buildings around his office, the dorms he is responsible for plumbing, cooling, and lighting. One of them butts up against the blast walls that separate our gym tent from the Iraqi dorms. Hisham stirs his tea and stands to walk back inside, away from the yelling and chanting of the trainees down the road. I follow him in with Hameed and put my tea glass down on his table. He hands me a stack of papers with diagrams of the dorms and highlighting in different colors, shakes my hand, and walks into the supply closet next to his office where he goes to pray. Hameed and I walk back to the Trailblazer. It's still before noon, but in mid-August it's already over 100 degrees.

"He's worried about the new commandos," Hameed says to me when we open the doors to let waves of hot air melt and ooze out of the car. "There's not enough space to put them in if they all finish."

I start the car and drive off the dirt parking area toward the road full of rock-wielding trainees. They live just behind the U.S. part of this compound, closest to the gun ranges. This class just started three days ago and Matt, who is their tactical U.S. adviser, tells me it's the first class where the Iraqis are really running the training. He and his team just make unexpected visits to make sure the training is effective and more or less legal by U.S. standards.

We pull up behind the line of trainees, and the instructor turns to me with an angry look. He unholsters his pistol a few inches, slams it back in, and then sees me. He yells something at his trainees, and they all run off the road into a dirt field and start to do push-ups next to their rocks. One of the trainees trips on the curb and drops his rock. This trainee has blond hair and no mustache and looks so different from his classmates I think he might be a U.S. plant. The instructor runs over to him and kicks him in the stomach as he tries to rise in a push-up. As we drive by, the instructor turns to me, one foot on the back of the blond trainee's neck, and smiles. Hameed sits in the passenger's seat; only his left shoulder moves up and down when he laughs. "See," he says. "They love you. All of them."

MATT KNOWS THAT WE WEREN'T REALLY TRAINED TO BE here, not like this at least, so he takes me out to the ranges a few times a week to work on my shooting and movement techniques. He has a special speed loader that fits over the top of an M4 magazine so you can load all thirty rounds simply by lining them up and depressing a plunger. It takes less than three seconds. We load a full rack, seven magazines, and ready three magazines for our 9mm. We leave the weapons in the truck and go staple targets to unstable wooden structures downrange. Some of them buckle under the weight of a green paper target and three staples.

"How long have these been here?" I ask Matt.

"Eight, maybe nine years," he says, kicking sand at the base of one to keep it upright.

Once the targets are more or less set up, we walk back to the truck, grab the ammo racks and guns, and walk to the line Matt kicks in the sand. We load and position our rifles at the low ready.

"Ready, up," Matt says and we take our rifles up, switch the selector off safe, fire three rounds into the targets, switch back to safe, and move to the low ready.

"Ready, right," Matt says, and we walk two targets right and fire.

We move left, back, forward, right, back, forward, left, and in little controlled boxes until we've emptied 210 rounds into the targets. When the 210th round of 5.56 leaves our M4s, we transition immediately to our 9mm and put three rounds into the target in front of us before we reholster the weapons and start the drill over with the sidearm. When we're empty, we drop the weapons back at the truck and look at the targets. I can tell which ones are Matt's bullets and which ones are mine. His cluster nicely toward the center of the green bust silhouette. Mine are in the shoulder, the top of the head, the bottom of the body, but they are on the target.

Matt smiles at me. "Fuck," he says. "You could actually be useful now. No more passing me your clips in a fight." He smiles at me and gives me a high five. "Your boyfriend will be so proud," he says and winks at me.

Somehow, without ever having discussed it, Matt knows I'm gay. I think it's because he is too, but even as we hear about Don't Ask Don't Tell's pending repeal, it is much scarier for him to be out than for me. These movement drills would be the perfect time to talk about it, since it's just the two of us on an otherwise empty gun range. But instead, we shoot holes in green paper and Matt occasionally brings up a boyfriend I don't have, usually in front of the rest of the team guys.

"Fuck you," I say.

We reload the racks and go again.

When we're done, we start cleaning up the ammo cans in the

back of his white Hilux truck. "We still need to get you back on the tower this month," he says.

A few months ago, when it became clear that I didn't know how to fast-rope out of a helicopter, Matt took me to the training tower and did drills with me. We spent every morning after breakfast on the tower until he was certain I could do it, should the need arise. Now we go every few weeks to maintain proficiency.

We hop in the car and get ready to leave the range. We drive with the windows down past the other ranges where groups of Iraqis are training. Matt waves at them. I wave at them.

"They fucking love you," Matt says.

The instructor unholsters his pistol a few inches, slams it back, and blows me a kiss.

MATT WORKS WITH BAKR, THE SCHOOLHOUSE'S GENERAL, almost daily. His job is to provide tactical advice for how to manage the pipeline of commandos. Despite the U.S. withdrawal only a few months away, hundreds of Iraqis volunteer for this unit. After the United States vets them and eliminates any with known nefarious backgrounds, they begin a selection process not unlike that which our own Green Berets go through. After eight years of occupation, what Matt and Bakr are finding out is that the Iraqis don't need much tactical advice. The United States has been running this pipeline long enough that enough Iraqis know how it works. What they need help with is logistics. Usually, what Bakr needs is something Hisham or one of the other Iraqis I work with has, but instead of asking them, or asking me, Bakr asks Matt to ask Perry. At first, they weren't getting food for lunch. Then they weren't getting food for dinner.

Perry has just learned I drove across the city in my Trailblazer, following a forklift that would only turn left, to bring them a water tank large enough so they could all shower on the same day.

"How'd you get that?" Perry asked me after I delivered the tank.

"I asked a unit leaving the country if I could have it."

"Well fuck," Perry said.

A six-foot-high mud wall separates the side where Perry and Sergeant Major Fuckface live with their guys, on the side with the gym, from my smaller air force team and the other Green Beret team we live with. There's a gate between the two, which Sergeant Major Fuckface has locked. To get to them, I have to walk out of our compound, around the back of the Iraqi dorms, through a break in the C-wire by the exploitation cell, and through a different gate they keep permanently open to the Iraqis. Matt lives on the gym side of the wall and is the only Green Beret who will come visit us over here. He walks into my office and sets one of the schoolhouse's new patches down on my desk. "General Bakr wanted you to have this to thank you for the water tank."

The patch has a burgundy border and a gray background. A burgundy eagle flies head-on in the center; the tips of his wings are white, black, and red to match the Iraqi flag. The eagle has two giant gold swords that look like the swords in the Hands of Victory in Baghdad in its claws, and an Iraqi flag in the middle. Some kind of green leafy branch makes a half circle, on the bottom, around the swords and eagle. Across the top, in English, are the letters ISWCS—Iraqi Special Warfare Center and School.

This is the only patch for the Iraqi units here I don't have. I have their old one, but Bakr has been stingy with giving out the new ones. Only the Iraqi instructors and Matt have them. It has Velcro on the back.

"You wanna come watch the training tomorrow morning? The head instructor asked for you. Said to bring *Jameela*."

MATT AND I DRIVE UP TO THE RANGE IN HIS WHITE PICKUP truck. They're at the farthest range from their dorms, the one closest to the twelve-foot mud wall that surrounds their base. We park and get out, and we walk over to stand under a canopy about fifteen feet behind the firing line. The instructor who was with the men carrying rocks is in front of the trainees and nods at Matt. The instructor turns around to shout instructions to the trainees.

"What are they learning?" I ask Matt.

"Stationary firing and basic movement techniques of the rifle."

The trainees set their rifles down on the ground and walk out to staple green targets to wooden supports, exactly the way we did this in New Jersey before we deployed. It's considerably more regimented than when Matt and I go shoot, but there are a lot more people with guns on this range. They walk back to their firing positions, and the instructor, standing downrange, gives them instructions.

"He shouldn't be doing that," Matt says and makes notes in his book.

The instructor unholsters his pistol a few inches, slams it back in, and moves to the other side of the firing line. He gives them more directions. They all pick up their rifles and load a magazine. The head instructor looks at his assistant standing behind the trainees and raises his hand into the air. The students begin to fire downrange at their green targets. After they shoot a few rounds, the trainees put down their rifles, and the assistant walks down the line to check the condition of their weapons. He nods to the head instructor, whose hand is still on his pistol. The students get up and walk downrange to look at their targets. The head instructor looks at each target, stops in front of the blond trainee's target, and begins to yell. He jabs his finger into the blond trainee's chest and points at the target, which evidently does not have the appropriate number of holes. The trainee next to him shows the instructor his target, apparently with too many holes. The instructor slaps him across the face and yells at the whole class.

"He's not supposed to do that," Matt says and writes something down.

As the instructor moves back and forth in front of the line of students, he points at the targets and at the blond trainee and the man next to him. Every time he reverses direction, he unholsters his pistol a few inches before slamming it back in.

The students walk back to the firing line and receive more directions.

"Do they wear ear plugs?" I ask Matt.

"They should." He points to a brand-new box of foam ear plugs that sits on a table next to me, behind the students, still plastic wrapped, and makes notes.

The students fire a few more rounds and walk back down-range to look at their targets. The instructor moves straight for the blond trainee, who slouches over when he reaches his target. The instructor shoves him from behind and pushes him into the target, knocking down the wooden structure. The trainee gets up and puts the target back upright, but the wood support broke, so it's crooked, cocked to the shooter's right.

"They're not supposed to do that," Matt says again. He walks over to the far left of the range, closer to the students but behind the firing line, and makes more notes.

As the students walk back to the firing line, the blond trainee says something to the man next to him, who nods. The instructor turns around and yells at the class, unholstering his pistol and reholstering it as he paces.

They shoot again, leave their rifles on the firing line, and walk downrange. Matt squats down, near the HESCO barriers on the left side of the range, in the shade. I take a few steps closer to stay in the shade of the canopy in the middle of the firing line. The instructor arrives at the blond's target before the blond does and stops. He puts his left hand on top of the cockeyed green paper stapled to 2x4s. Then he grabs the target to his right and puts his other hand on top of it. The students stand in front of their targets waiting for instructions. The assistant stands in front of the far-right target, five or six down from the head instructor, and waits.

The head instructor lets go of both targets and turns around. He says something to the blond recruit, who kneels down in front of him. The instructor faces the left side of the range and the right. He yells. The students yell an answer to him in unison. He yells. He paces over one target to the left, and then to the right, and then back to stand in front of the blond student. Then he blows me a kiss with his left hand. He yells. The blond student turns around and looks at me.

The instructor unholsters his pistol, points it at the back of the blond student's head, cocks the hammer, uncocks the hammer, and hits him with the gun.

His body twists back around and falls face-first into the dirt at the instructor's feet. He steadies himself on his hands when the instructor kicks him and walks away. He lies on the ground before coming to all fours, then to one knee.

"Fuck," Matt says and gets up. "Fuck."

The instructor reholsters his pistol, looks up at me, and smiles.

7

Elhamdullah

ADEL NEVER SPEAKS TO ME IN ENGLISH, BUT HE UNDER-stands me when I talk to him, and he knows what I tell Hameed. He also knows someone told me a few months ago that Adel's English has improved drastically over the last three years, in part because of the school in Texas the United States sent him to, and also in part because of the woman he met there and report-edly married, and to whom he sends flowers on Thursdays. Adel is grateful my knowledge of this has not affected my opinion of him. We play soccer with Adel's battalion on Fridays. Beck and I are the only two Americans who have played soccer before, and despite their years of training and unbelievable physical fit-ness, Green Berets have a distinct eye-foot coordination problem. During the games, the strategy on our side is to simply outrun the Iraqis, and when that fails, to employ brute physical force. We win every tackle we make. The Iraqi strategy is their reliance on their knowledge of the game, which for these men, is instinctual. They have been juggling a ball as long as they have been walk-ing, which means they can pass with both feet, trap a ball out of the air, and make a first touch that doesn't send the ball fifteen yards in front of them. We lose every game we play.

At first, Adel must have told his guys to take it easy on us, and the team that started was clearly made up of the older, fatter members of the unit. Hazbar, the Iraqi battalion's elder states-man, made an appearance, much to the delight of the men in the battalion twenty years his junior. He was terrible, but still better than all of us. On our side, Beck and I tried to assign loose positions to people (offense, defense, goalie), but eventually we gave up and let whoever wanted to run around the field until exhaustion. We played the entire first half of our first game with thirteen players and were still losing at halftime. Sabrina, my personnel specialist responsible for conducting background investigations of the Iraqi soldiers we live with, biometrically cataloging them, and issuing them access badges for U.S. installations, played offense, which essentially meant we didn't expect her to run back past midfield ever. Once the Iraqis were up 3–0, they stopped running. They let Sabrina dribble the ball the length of the field from her starting position at midfield, straight down the middle, bouncing the ball ten to fifteen yards ahead of her as she ran behind it. When she got inside the penalty box, the Iraqi goalie ran sideways out of the net. The entire battalion chanted, "*Baget malta! Baget malta!*"—"My badge! My badge!"—and clapped their hands. Sabrina lined up her strike, swung her foot through, and sent the ball wide to the left, missing the goal entirely. It seemed the entire Iraqi team dropped in unison to the dirt, hands on their heads. I heard one of them say, "Lean forward, open your eyes, don't blink"—instructions for the biometric iris scanner—as he walked past her to set up for the goal kick.

Yesterday, when we played the battalion, Adel wasn't there. We were down 9–0 before halftime. Sean, an overly excited weapons sergeant from the team we live with who made rank far too quickly, did not tolerate our humiliation well. He began running full speed into the Iraqis, whether the ball was there or not. As the coach, this Iraqi battalion's U.S. adviser, and the only officer, I subbed him out, which only made him angrier and caused him to run off the field back to the U.S. compound on the other side of the Iraqi base where, I'm told, he donned his body armor and ran another six miles. Soon after I dismissed Sean, the Iraqi center back tried to clear the ball from the back but shanked it off the side of his foot. It bounced once in front of me, and then I took it off a chest trap and lined up on the half-volley. The ball, like it was suddenly rocket propelled, launched into the upper right corner of the goal. It was so unexpected the entire Iraqi battalion stood frozen in place after it happened. We celebrated as though we had just qualified for the World Cup. I ran around the field zigzagging like an airplane, then ran to the rest of my team, who gathered at midfield chanting, "U-S-A! U-S-A!" Their goalie and center back subbed themselves out and left the dirt field. We lost the game 17–1, but it felt like we won.

Friday football games have become such a regular occurrence that Adel's men now plan their leave to make sure they are present for them. When I go to see Adel now, the TV in his office that used to stream *Al Jazeera* now shows highlights from the Qatari soccer league. As I sit in his office today, I comment on the goals as they cycle through the highlights. One of the players scores on a half-volley off a bad clearance. I point to the TV and tell him that's how I scored. "*Na'am, na'am,*" he says. He knows all about it from his men. He gets up from his desk and zigzags around his office, arms extended like an airplane, and laughs.

"*Quwat jaweed,*" I say (air force), shrug my shoulders, and smile.

He sits back down and pages someone from the hall. One of the boys he employs to brew and bring us chai enters the room holding a gold trophy draped in a silk scarf with the unit's name and patch on it. The chai boy places the trophy on the desk in front of Adel and walks to the door to leave, hands extended like an airplane.

"But we'll never win," I say to Adel and smile. Hameed translates but doesn't have to.

Adel laughs and says as Hameed interprets, "Then it's good it looks nice in here."

He says on Friday he'll bring the trophy with him. We'll all take a picture with it before the game. I agree. Then he moves the trophy to the other side of his desk to tell me he was selected to attend the NATO Counterterrorism School in Germany. In English, he says, "I can't go without my adviser."

Hameed interprets this into Arabic and looks at me. "Wait," Hameed says, also disarmed by the language shift. I tell Adel that

I will talk to the army guy I work for and see if I am allowed to go with him. He calls for chai, and we watch some more high-lights. After we finish our chai, Hameed and I get up to leave. As we walk out, I extend my hands like an airplane and hear Adel laugh as we close the door.

AT THE OPERATIONS MEETINGS THAT ARE RUN EVERY NIGHT but Friday by the teams I work for, I wait patiently as they cycle through slides of the targets they are tracking, the new intelligence they have on certain leaders of known Iranian-backed militias, and plans for tonight's operations. I jot down notes about some of the logistics and watch with interest as their explosive ordinance specialist tells us about the new tactics Iraqis are using to kill Americans on the roads. Recently, they have started position-ing improvised explosives on overpasses pointed down in con-junction with daisy-chained buried devices. When they detonate, they go right through the turrets and roofs of convoy vehicles, rendering all the armor and reinforced undercarriages useless. The only other air force person outside my team that works with this unit is their Joint Terminal Air Controller (JTAC), a staff sergeant in charge of calling in air strikes from the ground. He doesn't come to most of the meetings, no one really knows where he goes, and we only see him when the teams meet for their pre-mission briefing. The last slide of the Ops and Intel meet-ing is usually devoted to a comical and obscene joke about their attempts to locate the JTAC. Tonight the final slide is a picture of Ronaldo running toward his team after scoring a goal, hands extended like an airplane. Superimposed over his face is a pic-ture of Kate Hudson's face, apparently the closest equivalent to me they could find. These men usually don't know what I do and generally don't care as long as they have bullets and batteries and paper for their giant map printer. But even they heard about the goal, and the fact that we scored—that I scored—and ended the Iraqi shutout is news worth celebrating.

At the end of the meeting, I approach Perry, the commander

of this unit, with Adel's request. "He says he can't go to the NATO school without his adviser," I say.

"Who's his adviser?" Perry asks.

"I am," I say. He frequently forgets I am this battalion's adviser because, as a B-52 aircraft maintenance officer serving here as a logistician embedded with two dozen Green Berets, I am the least qualified person for this job.

"Okay," Perry says, and he gives me the name of the person at the central task force to work with on my temporary duty assignment orders to Germany. "By the way," he says as I go to leave, "nice work on the goal. Bet it eats them that a girl ended their shutout streak." He grabs a handful of almonds, leans back in his desk chair, and laughs.

IF YOU GO IN GATE NUMBER TWO OF THE VICTORY BASE Complex and turn right, eventually you'll end up at Camp Liberty or Camp Victory. I still don't know the difference, except that one of them serves decent barbecue on Wednesdays. Go left inside Gate Number Two, and eventually you find the U.S. Special Forces compound, where some of the people I work for live, and the blank gate with quiet, sleepy Ugandans who are supposed to write down the letter on the keys we give them to pass, but never do. Instead, they tip their floppy-brimmed hats and wait for their turn to take the bus to the American-run dining hall for all-they-can-eat steak and lobster on Mondays.

I've tried for months to work with VBC's defense operations center to make the process of our Iraqis coming through Gate Number Two more fluid. They all, thanks to Sabrina, have access badges. Their vehicles are registered with the base. They announce their movement through Gate Number Two hours in advance. Still there are problems, particularly when they come back with detainees. Last night, when they came through Gate Number Two with a detainee—an enormously large woman who, we later learned, was hiding thumb drives in her fat rolls—one of the commandos from the battalion's small commando company found an M9 pistol near the clearing barrel at the gate. Thinking it belonged to someone in the convoy, he picked it up. When the convoy returned to our base here at the end of the mission and handed off the obese detainee to the interrogation cell (she almost crushed one of the guards as she dismounted the gun truck in handcuffs), they did a weapon inventory. None of them had lost a weapon. They then conducted an inventory by serial number of all the weapons in the brigade, some two thousand in all. They finished right before the sun came up, and they were not missing an M9 pistol.

Adel calls me early, and Hameed and I go to meet him. When we get to his office, we find the pistol, cleared, safe, sitting on his desk next to the trophy. He explains what happened, how they found it near Gate Number Two, how they checked all the weapons in the brigade, and it's not theirs. He tells me he thinks it belongs to an American, maybe one of the guards who stands at Gate Number Two and demands to see the colorful plastic ID cards Sabrina issues. I take down the serial number and tell him I can find out. He calls for chai and apologizes for meeting with me so early. It is 8:30 a.m. While we sip chai, we watch the highlights from yesterday's Champions League games. Ronaldo runs across the screen, and I think of Kate Hudson.

When I get back to my office, I call the base defense operations center and ask if anyone has reported a lost weapon. In fact, one of the guards at the gate did report his weapon missing after his shift. I ask for them to verify the serial number. The man on the phone refuses, citing security concerns. "We will send someone to get the weapon," he says.

"You will not," I say. We are guarded about who we let on this base, in part because it is an Iraqi base. But we are also leery because some of the things necessary for successful special operations are not viewed favorably by the regular army. We have had the Office of Special Investigation, Army Criminal Investigation Division, and FBI attempt to enter the base without authorization. All of them were turned away by the guy with a machine gun at the first gate. Entry onto our compound is sometimes viewed as a badge of honor for people who don't live here. Most people who get in tell people it is because they had business to conduct with the U.S. Special Forces. Most of those people are lying. We do our business here. If it involves others, we go to them, which is what I tell the man on the phone. I also tell him that it was an Iraqi who found the lost weapon, so the Iraqi will be delivering it.

"Iraqis aren't allowed to have weapons on our post," the man says.

"He will be unarmed, except for the empty weapon you lost," I say.

"We will detain him if you aren't with him," he says.

"You realize that doesn't make sense, don't you?" I ask.

"You can drop it off between 1600 and 1700, accompanying the Iraqi, or don't come at all," he says.

"If we don't come at all," I say, "you still have a lost weapon."

He hangs up the phone. Adel calls Hameed to ask what he can do to return the lost weapon to the Americans. Hameed tells him that we need to return it between 1600 and 1700, and that I must go with him. He says that is fine, but he will need to run a few errands afterward. He will meet me outside the large steel door of our U.S. area at 1500, and we can drive together. I agree. Hameed tells me he has something to do then and can't go with us. "What do you have to do?" I ask him.

"You know," he says and shrugs. We work together from 9:00 a.m. until about 1:00 p.m., then again from around 10:00 p.m. until two or three in the morning, so it seems reasonable for him to do things at other times, even though I don't actually know what those things are. Adel speaks enough English so that we can manage, and I don't mind silence. Later I will find out that one of the explicit guidelines set forth by the U.S. commander in Iraq is that one can never be alone with an Iraqi. I am supposed to take at least two other U.S. service members with me. (I would only need one if I were a man.) But I also know that if I bring two other people with me, it will look like I don't trust Adel.

And while I don't entirely, breaching the trust we do have will do more than cancel Friday football games. I tell Schwab I'm going with Adel. He says okay and reaffirms that he will take over if I am kidnapped or killed, and he asks if he will get promoted to captain if that happens.

Adel arrives on time and with the weapon, which he hands me. I wave at Schwab who, ever since my most trendiest haircut ever, has taken to singing the chorus to the Indigo Girls' "Closer to Fine" whenever he is around me. He closes the door behind us, and I get into Adel's car and we drive. We are headed to the place with the good barbecue on Wednesdays, which I have only been to a few times. Adel turns on the radio as we drive. We tune into the American Forces Network station. Madonna's "Like a Prayer" comes on, and Adel turns up the volume. I nod my head along with the song and look out the window at the lowering Iraqi sun. Adel starts singing along faintly. As the song builds, he gets more confident and sings louder. I start singing with him. He smiles and turns up the volume. He looks at me and rolls down the windows, and we both belt out the lyrics.

We sway back and forth in his gold Mitsubishi Pajero, alternating the lyrics at the end. As the song tapers off, we laugh and smile and forget for a minute that I am part of a force occupying his country, that he is a member of an elite unit charged with eliminating the threats within his own people, and that we are delivering a lost weapon to people who have been in charge of the occupation for eight years and manage it by hanging up on people trying to help them.

Adel turns down the radio, a commercial comes on, and he changes the station to Hayati FM. Arabic pop is a strange genre. Some of the songs sound American, except for the harshness of the Arabic language and the unfamiliar rhymes. Some songs are laced with the stringed rhythms you would expect a belly dancer to replicate with her hips and jingled skirt. I've learned that Nancy and Fares Karam, both Lebanese, are chart toppers right now. I recognize none of Nancy's songs, but I do know she is the only female spokesperson for Coca-Cola in the Middle East. Fares Karam's music is not quite as poppy as Nancy's and employs more of the traditional sounds of Lebanon. I received his CD, *Elhamdullah*, meaning praise or thanks be to Allah, as a gift. It, along with knowledge of Adel's wife in Texas, are what Sarkis left me with when I dropped him off at the Baghdad International Airport terminal one Thursday morning back in March. The music is catchy, and I find myself learning the sounds of the words and trying to interpret the strings with gyrations of my hips, particularly of the CD's title track, "Elhamdullah."

I point to where Adel needs to turn to cross the river, and he signals the change of course. We pass an American convoy, and every soldier sitting near a window stares at us as we drive by, Adel with one hand on the wheel, one hand held over his head trying to block the drooping sun. I sit in the passenger seat with an empty lost pistol on my lap and look out the side window away from the sun. I point to the building we need to park in front of, and Adel turns in, parks, and shuts off the car. We get out and walk up to a heavily barricaded door. I tuck my shirt over my pistol, hip-holstered, loaded, and mostly out of sight. Adel brushes off the front of his uniform. I lock the slide of the empty pistol to the rear. A small slit in the steel door opens, and I tell a pair of eyes I am here to speak with the O-5, their commander, a lieutenant colonel in the U.S. Army. The slit closes, the door opens, and we are escorted in, tracked by unarmed soldiers panicking in the presence of a real live Iraqi. They don't know we sang along to Madonna on the way over. They don't know that Adel leads what is very likely the only unit in Iraq that would have actually returned a found American weapon. They don't know about his English or his wife in San Antonio.

When we arrive at the O-5's office, he motions us in and proceeds to read me my rights. Normally this would alarm me. But I learned months ago that my best chance of survival here is to ignore normal responses to events I have developed elsewhere in my adult life. Adel stands behind me and to my left, hands folded in front of him, and stares at the ground. His posture is that of a servant awaiting reproach. "Please state how you came upon the stolen weapon," the O-5 says.

"Please verify the serial number of the lost weapon," I say back.

He works me over with his eyes. "Are you armed, Captain?" he asks.

"Please verify the serial number of the missing weapon," I say back. Perry tried to warn me about the regular army. They are so large, and so broken by eight years of trying to occupy, destroy, and then rebuild a country, that very often they confuse the order of the natural world. Perry told me not to trust them farther than I could throw them, and because of the good barbecue on Wednesdays, that is not far.

"Please state how you came upon the stolen weapon," the O-5 says again.

"Please verify the serial number of the lost weapon," I say.

"Goddamn it, Captain! You know damn well they stole it from us. Why the hell did you bring him?" He points to Adel, who, fully understanding the words the O-5 is yelling, remains unmoved.

"His men found the lost weapon," I say. "After conducting a brigade-wide inventory of their own weapons, they determined it was not theirs. At which point, they began to actively seek its owner. Your own unit could learn from their diligent accountability practice."

The O-5 moves six feet to his left to find a desk to crush with both of his fists. Tobacco leaks slowly out of the right side of his mouth. Spit flies forward as he speaks to me. "What the fuck! What the fuck do you know about weapon accountability? Do you fucking count airplanes to make sure you didn't lose any? Do you even fucking know where the serial number is on an M9? Have you ever even fucking fired one? I'm telling you these same haji bastards stole our goddamn pistol, and you're here telling me how to fucking count? Who's your fucking supervisor?"

"Which one?" I ask. It seems like a legitimate question. I work for any one of eight people, so even I don't entirely know how I might answer that.

"What the fuck!" he says again and smashes the desk. "You don't even know? I bet you work for that fucktard who told me I would be detained at the gate if I tried to come there myself."

"Perry?" I ask.

"Fuck!" he says and grabs the edge of the desk and wipes the stream of dip from his face. He moves a piece of paper and reads me the six-digit number. I check it against the pistol in my hand, walk forward, and place it on the desk. I turn around to face Adel.

"Is it over?" he asks me in English.

"*Na'am, saydie. Yallah,*" I say, and we walk away from the trembling O-5. As we make our way down the hall, I hear him behind me yell, "Motherfucking air force cunt waltzes in here with some haji motherfucker and tells me how to fucking count."

We get back in Adel's car as the sun sets. Before he turns it on, he looks at me and says, "Dinner? I have . . . idea."

He starts the car and we drive away from the O-5, the defense operations center, and the regular army. Adel reaches into the back seat and hands me a dishdasha and scarf. He is taking me to dinner in Baghdad, and while I have on tan boots, this will at least make me less obvious. I put the dishdasha over my uniform, smooth it out, and wrap my head while he drives. At the restaurant he, still in uniform, leads us through a back entrance and upstairs to the roof. He is friends with the waiter, who brings us a pot of chai, *samoon*, and hummus. Adel orders kebobs for us. As we eat, we don't talk. Instead, we look past each other into the lights of Baghdad. Behind him are some high rises that stretch along the river. If I didn't know better, it could be San Antonio.

We get another pot of chai and Adel tries to pay, but the waiter wants only a photo with me, which he takes; he then leaves our table, hands extended behind him like an airplane. Adel chuckles as we walk down the stairs to his car. Even the waiter knows.

As we drive back, Adel turns the radio up enough to cut the silence. We drive with the windows open once we are back on a road without many cars. I take off the dishdasha and scarf, fold them, and set them on the back seat. Just before we make the turn to head for the front of our base, "Elhamdullah" comes on the radio.

"I love this song!" I say and turn it up. I often think I should look up, or ask Hameed to translate, the words. I practice the sounds to them just in case I am somewhere where it might be useful to be able to sound like I can speak one stanza of Arabic. So I sing along.

Adel laughs and turns up the radio louder. He sings the next verse. I sing what I think are the right sounds for the next verse, and we alternate this way until the song is over. He turns down the radio. "You are good," he says. "But you should practice this verse." Then he recites:

Rjh'le mbarha law feek wa'efli borka el jaye
Bkafee tehlam ya shreek haldenye elha nhaye
O'llo allah elhamdullah
Wel se-ha mneeha
Elhamdullah

I try it but stumble over the first sound. We try again and I make it through the first line. We do the second. We practice twice more as the car pulls up in front of the U.S. part of the Iraqi base. He parks the car and gets out.

"I'm sorry that guy was so horrible," I say.

Adel laughs and shrugs. "*Shukran, Jameela,*" he says and gives me a hug.

"*Ma'a salama, sadiki,*" I say (goodbye, my friend), and I walk through the gate. Hameed and Schwab are sitting on the patio waiting for me. Disappointed he won't be promoted, Schwab tells me he's glad I'm back and leaves.

"Hameed," I say before he goes too. "What does '*rjh'le mbarha law feek wa'efli borka e jaye, bkafee tehlam ya shreek haldenye elha nhaye'* mean?"

"Oh, from the song," he says. "It means something like 'bring back yesterday and stop tomorrow from coming; enough dreaming my friend, this world has an end.'"

8

Cartography

EVERY TIME HE COMES TO THIS PART OF THE DESERT, JADE tells me, he gives himself a new tattoo. He's done this since the commander he advises was a captain, when he and his guys lived in tents and undertook most of the operations on their own, without the help of the Iraqis, which would be eight or nine rotations ago, eight years. On their first rotation, he had only black ink, and the tattoo scabbed. He's learned to deploy with a full kit.

"We can do it in the team room," Jade says. "Come on, I'll show you."

To get from the operations center to the team room, we go through a steel door with no handle or lock, through a wooden door with a large steel keypad and two locks, and through another wooden door with an elaborate entry keypad. Jade is the team sergeant for one of the teams I work with. Now we live with the Iraqis, train with them, and advise them. I am trying to establish the Iraqi commander's logical infrastructure. But I am in the team room because Jade thinks that I should get a tattoo.

Their team room is full of screens, maps, cubbies of bulletproof vests, helmets, night vision devices, different optics for rifles, extra magazines, loose rounds of ammunition, face shields, buckets of bazooka bubble gum. In the center of the room is a huge rectangular table. It is at least twelve feet long, four feet wide, and of everything in this compound, it is most likely to survive an aerial attack. It is covered in maps with green and red highlighted routes of travel, purple dots marking known targets and sources, a sheet with radio frequencies, call signs, and code words. In the middle of all these maps, which frame the edges of the table and sit half covered by a pane of glass not quite big enough, is a five-foot-tall, three-foot-wide poster of a woman entirely naked except for a pair of shoes and a bandolier that sits between her obviously augmented breasts. Her legs are spread, her toes pointed out in red heels, her gaze is slightly off center to the right, her long blond hair responds to an invisible breeze. She clutches a Barrett sniper rifle by the barrel, angled between her legs, hands clasped right above the lower receiver, guiding the rest of the barrel toward her clean-shaven pink upper receiver, the muzzle break less than an inch away. The iron front sight is up. Above her head, in white letters standing out against the blackness behind her, is the phrase "Lightweight Bolt Carrier."

From where I stand, she appears to be looking directly at me from her flat position on the table. Jade wanders to his cubby and waves me over. He shows me his setup. One professional tattoo machine gun; two different types of power supply; a foot pedal; a case of colorful inks, with an emphasis on the blue family; a stack of sterile tattoo needles seven inches thick; at least fifty ink cups; a box of black nitrile gloves, size large (the same gloves we order for the medic kits); a container of white needle tips; one bottle of H2Ocean tattoo recovery cream.

"See, we can do you right on the table if you want, depending on where you want the tat," he says.

"I don't think I want a tat," I say.

He shows me the blue flames that go up his left arm and form the special forces shield in slightly darker blue flames, then turn into blue smoke that forms their team shield. He designed it himself and had Aaron ink it. If you didn't know better, they'd just be flickering blue flames. On his left forearm is a green dancing leprechaun smoking a fat brown cigar and winking. "Think about it," he says.

"I will." Then I ask about their map printer, which has been malfunctioning for three months. In fact, the only thing it has successfully printed since it arrived in this country was the Lightweight Bolt Carrier adorning the middle of their table. Even though I've never seen one before, someone suggested I look at the giant printer and try to fix it. Jade points me to it and leaves me with the checklist of parts I found for it on the internet. My strategy with the $7,000 42-inch wide-capacity printer is to make sure each part is here, and if not, order the missing one in hopes that it fixes whatever malfunction exists. When I tell Jade this is my strategy, as I have never seen a map printer before, he seems impressed.

"Wouldn't have thought of that," he says. "Guess that's why they give us air force people. What do you do for the air force anyway?" He sits down by the Lightweight Bolt Carrier's left high heel and sketches Aaron's new tattoo, a skeleton with what looks like a hula-hoop, a tiara, and a magic wand.

"I'm an aircraft maintenance officer on the B-52."

"Huh." He sketches a skeleton elephant next to the hula-hooping, tiara-wearing skeleton. The team door opens behind us.

"Whoa!" Perry says when he walks into the team room and sees me.

"Whoa," says Jade when he looks up and sees Perry. He places a map over his sketch and looks instead at randomly placed purple dots. He later tells me that the commander rarely comes into the team rooms, except when he's rolling on a mission with the team.

"Hi, sir," I say and look back at the manual I have for the printer. I realize that the entire manual is in only four languages: Japanese (or Chinese?), Chinese (or Japanese?), Korean, and another language I cannot identify but is made up of phrases like: Pastikan orientasi kertas sesuai dengan arah yang ditunjukkan. My inventory of printer parts proceeds based entirely on pictures.

"What are you doing in here?" he asks me.

"I'm looking at the printer," I say.

He nods. "How many boxes of SureFire batteries do we have on hand?" he asks Jade.

"Six," I say, because these are the things I know.

"Six," Jade says and circles something on the map.

"Huh," Perry says as he tries to move a stack of papers over the woman's upper receiver.

"Listen," he says to me once he has covered her to his satisfaction, "I'm glad you're here. We need you at dinner tonight."

The dinner he means is one that happens every week with the Iraqi general we all support and the sheikhs of the communities around us. Tonight, the sheikh of Abu Ghraib is coming, as well as the sheikh of the Shuala district, and apparently someone close to Muqtada al-Sadr. I can't think why I might be needed at dinner. The first time I went, having been in the country for less than forty-eight hours, I was escorted to the back room, where the general's wife and her friends ate the meal with his children. Sarkis left me there so he and the guy I had replaced could receive the gifts the general was giving them (which included a ten-foot-by-ten-foot handwoven silk rug, a tea set, and a pair of sunglasses evidently from New Year's 2002). Since I was unable to speak to any of the women, one of them handed me a baby and smiled as I sat there pretending to know what to do with a baby in the back room of a palace that used to be Saddam's zoo outside of Baghdad. On a TV mounted on a mantle above a fake fireplace, *Austin Powers* played in English. Above the TV was a portrait of the Iraqi general in his traditional Kurdish clothing kneeling in the snows of Arbil, one arm around a baby goat, the other arm holding an AK-47.

The general's wife who handed me the baby wore a lace-up white shirt, similar to what I imagine pirates wearing as they hunted the open seas for Spanish treasure ships. Her breasts were nearly as large as the Lightweight Bolt Carrier's and equally fake. My interpreter later told me these were Lebanese breasts because Lebanon is the place to go for breast augmentation if you live in this area. He said he could set up an appointment with someone he knew, were I interested.

Over the woman's lace shirt was a black leather vest that stopped just short of the top of her bright red A-line skirt. She wore stockings with butterflies fluttering about in the pattern. Her lips, perhaps also Lebanese, seemed always to be pursed and were adorned in bright red to match her skirt. She wore gold-glittered wedge heels, four or five inches high, that had gold straps wrapped up to the base of her calves. Her friends wore similar outfits with variations in the sizes of their Lebanese augmentations and in the colors of their skirts. Everyone's lips exactly matched at least one component of her wardrobe.

The baby started to cry and began grabbing things on my uniform. I turned it around so it wouldn't rip off my name tag, and it started to kick generally in the direction of my holstered, concealed pistol. Unlike many air force members elsewhere in this country, I wear a hip holster because Jade and Aaron have instructed me that anyone who wears a shoulder holster never plans on using his pistol. I moved the baby to the other side of my lap. A small semicircle of coordinated lipstick shades sat evaluating my lack of parenting skills before the baby's mother quickly took it back. Bouncing on its mother's lap, the baby stopped crying. As if alerted to the awkward silence that overtook us, a small monkey ran full speed into one of the translucent yellow windows behind the women, its face smashed fully into the glass, its palms flat with fingers extended. I could have counted its teeth. I jumped a bit on one of the couches. The baby started crying, and the pirate woman with Lebanese breasts turned to the window and shrieked, "Mojo! Mojo! Mojo!" Dr. Evil and Mini-Me began to rap "It's a Hard Knock Life" on the TV to my left.

After that first dinner, I decided it best never to return, but trying to figure out what part of that experience I might be able to convey to Perry, I give up, return to my picture inventory, and ask what time we need to leave.

I MEET PERRY AT THE TRUCK TO DRIVE TO THE GENERAL'S house, and he looks me over, head to foot. I am the only one here in a uniform. All the Green Berets are wearing whatever they want, which is generally a combination of old T-shirts from various races and athletic events, pants made out of some kind of technical material that promotes moisture wicking, and sturdy trail-running shoes. Perry is wearing a collared shirt. He has mentioned to me before that I should wear something else. When I ask him what would be appropriate, he pauses, looks at Brandon, one of the team leaders, looks at me, and then tells me to just wear my uniform.

I ride in the back seat with Jade, who has brought his sketchbook of tattoos he's giving guys on the teams. Aaron, in addition to getting the tiara skeleton and elephant skeleton, will also get the skeleton of a monkey. The JTAC is getting a tattoo of the outline of one of the prisoners of Abu Ghraib made famous by scandal, posed with hands extended by his side, a hood over his head, and wearing what appears to be a dress. The image is filled in with various shades of blue raindrops. KP is getting the footprint of his second daughter and the opposite foot of his first daughter, so that the two footprints appear to be walking. Jade tells me that the first footprint is just below KP's heart, and the second one will be walking a path up to his shoulder. Someone else on the team is getting a cartoonish barbell, flexed under its own load and smiling. Frank, the intelligence sergeant on the team, who knows more about what is happening in Iraq than anyone else in the south of this country, is getting a poker hand (full house, sevens over twos) put on the left side of his ribcage.

We arrive at dinner and we walk in, one interpreter among the six of us: Perry, Brandon, Jade, Frank, KP, and me. The general greets us and brings us into his house, past the large front room, which has a small pond that flows in from the lake outside. Grazing near the place where we parked the truck are two African oryxes and a cage containing three white peacocks. Sitting on the railing surrounding the pond, in the great room of this palace, is a large bird of prey, tethered to the rail with a small shackle around its right foot. Above the bird's head is a clock. The hands of the clock tick counterclockwise. In the center of the clock is a small team of commandos ready to breach a door. Once in the back room with the opaque yellow windows, Jody, the general's chai boy, brings us a round of chai. I sit opposite the general and the sheikhs, on the end of the same couch I sat on the first time I was here, with Jade to my right, Brandon to his right. I watch the window for the monkey. Hussein enters the room and joins the chai circle. There is nowhere for him to sit, so the general looks at me, waves his hand, and says, "*Yallah.*"

I look at Perry, who sits to the general's left. He shrugs and says, "I think they can all fit." Karam, their interpreter, suggests this to the general, who then motions with his hands to make room on our couch for Hussein. Brandon and Jade shift right, and I follow them over. Jade shoots left-handed, so his pistol and mine clank together, concealed by layers of clothes. I lean back as far as I can so his is more accessible. Hussein squeezes himself onto the couch to my left and puts his arm around me. "*Naqueeb Jameela,*" he says and smooths his mustache. The men all lean forward and discuss.

One of the sheikhs speaks in a very low mumbled tone and covers his mouth. He stares directly at me the entire time but is careful to make sure I cannot hear him, though I can't understand him anyway. When Karam interprets, the sheikh has instructed him to speak the same way. Perry looks at me and says, "Bullets and M2 gun barrel parts," and motions for me to write this down. I wiggle around on the couch to get out a notebook and pen. In the process, Hussein hugs me and laughs. The general laughs a little too, then smooths his mustache.

Everyone begins speaking in an even lower voice, and Jade and Brandon scoot our couch closer to the other so they may better hear. Hussein puts up his arm in front of me, as though he were arresting my motion toward the windshield in a car stopping short. I lean back and watch the window for the monkey. The general takes out a yellow folder and sets it on the table between us. Perry points at me. I get ready to write something down, but he waves me off and points to the folder. The general nods. Hussein smooths his mustache. The sheikh smooths his mustache. Perry has no mustache but smooths his upper lip. Everyone stands up and starts to shake hands. Hussein turns to me, says my name again, gives me a hug, and takes the folder. We walk to a different room to eat dinner around a large table with no plates or silverware.

"You have a meeting with Hussein and some of the regional battalion commanders tonight at midnight," Perry tells me when Hussein leaves to get me a banana for dessert.

"What is the meeting about?" I ask him.

"Something about how they are having trouble getting gun parts for their .50 cals, and they are short on ammunition for the 240. I told him you might be able to help," he says and eats another dolma.

"What made you think I would be able to help?" I ask him.

"I don't know. It just seems like it's what you do. Plus, I figured it would get him off my back for a while so I could talk to the sheikh."

Hussein returns with a banana and peels it for me before he presents it with a modest bow. "*Shukran, saydie*," I say and take the banana.

He laughs and smooths his mustache. He has a daughter my age, in addition to the older one he showed me a picture of, but he doesn't get to see her much. When I finally ask him about her, he shows me photos that he keeps concealed in his desk drawer, and one under the chess set on the table in his office. He will give me 90,000 dinar and ask me to buy her American shampoo again because, he tells me again, she deserves better than what Iraq can offer her.

After dinner the men go back to meet with the sheikhs, and I wander outside with the caged peacocks and oryxes. A horse is tethered next to the peacock cage, apparently just back from a good gallop. Jody, the chai boy—who is almost fifty—has a son that exercises this horse. I watch as the boy—a boy of about eleven—dips a brush in cool water and runs it over the horse's coat. One of the peacocks fans his tail and parades for me in his cage. The fanned tail of a white peacock looks a bit like a dandelion, waiting for a wish to be made and then to be blown away. When he is done with his dance, he draws down his tail, turns, and walks away. From behind, he looks like a tiny avalanche lurching forward in the Mesopotamian desert.

I don't know how long I watch him, but the men return and we get back into the truck and drive away. "That would be a good tattoo," Jade says. "A peacock. But you'd want the regular one. Not one of those weird white ones."

"I think I like the white ones better," I say. "They remind me of snow." Then I lean back and have a nap the rest of the way back to our compound, dreaming about skiing the deep, light Colorado snow on Red Mountain Pass. Perry lets me out and reminds me of my meeting with Hussein; then he and his guys drive back to plan a mission or a new tattoo.

Back at our camp, I tell Hameed about the meeting. "Where is it?" he asks.

"I don't know," I say. But I tell him to meet me at 11:45 p.m. and we'll go to wherever it is together. I have two hours to figure out where the meeting is and how to help Hussein and the outstation commanders with their problem without having ever actually attempted to order spare parts for a .50 cal before. There is no part book I can find on the internet either.

I walk back to the side of our compound where Jade's team room is to ask where this meeting might take place. No one is in the operations center when I come by, so I decide to walk into Jade's team room. I knock first, but when no one answers I open the door with the code Jade slipped me. Jade sits across the table, near the woman's feet, with Aaron in an adjacent chair, skeletons stenciled onto his forearm. Brandon flips through a *Maxim* to Jade's right. Everyone freezes, Jade midmotion assembling the tattoo gun, and stares at me. Another one of the team guys, whom I don't know well, cranes his head out from behind the cubbies and stares.

"I was just hoping someone would know where my meeting

with Hussein is tonight," I say without walking in far enough to make eye contact with the woman on the table.

"The ITOC," a voice from behind the cubbies says. I shut the door and leave. Behind me I hear the constant low buzz of Jade's tattoo machine firing up.

WHEN I MEET HAMEED AT 11:45 TO DRIVE TO THE IRAQI Tactical Operations Center, bats flutter around the camouflage canopy where he sits, flashing in front of the lights in varying-sized winged specks. Hameed sits on the bench under the netting and watches the bats take turns launching themselves into the night from the top of a twelve-foot concrete blast wall behind him, which divides our part of this base from the Iraqis'.

"How was dinner?" he asks me.

"He has peacocks," I say. "White ones."

We walk out the gate, get to the car, and start to drive toward the ITOC. It is a concrete building with no windows, poor air conditioning, and inconsistent power because the Iraqis choose to hoard the fuel we give them for the generator rather than keep the building constantly lit. The sheep that Hazbar raises for his brother's kabob restaurant live between the heavily guarded ITOC generator and the butcher shop, unaware that they graze between the two houses that meticulously plot death. The ITOC is where, after carefully watching people and learning their patterns and habits, the Iraqis plan missions to show up at the targets' houses in the middle of the night, kick down their doors, and extract them. I am more regularly involved in the butcher shop's operation than the ITOC's and its secret plans and execution orders, so I know where it is only because Hazbar pointed it out the last time we had dinner and talked about how we might find a bull-dozer and a front loader for him.

Hameed and I arrive at the ITOC a little before midnight and park between a date tree nearly ready for harvest and a few sheep, napping in the dirt parking lot, that do not move to accommodate the car. We walk inside the building and weave down the concrete halls covered with pictures of Iraqi commandos who have died helping Americans. At the mission room, we knock on the heavy steel door and are welcomed by Hussein, three men I do not know, and two rounds of chai. Hussein points at a chart displayed on the TV screen, hands me the yellow folder, and yells. In normal conversation, Hussein yells. The only exceptions are when he says my name and when he whispers in Arabic into my ear, asking me to marry him and keep his house in Diyala. Though now sometimes even the Diyala proposals seem to be shouted. Later, when he tells me more about his daughter, he will speak softly; otherwise, he yells.

The three strangers yell back. Hameed has not translated anything, and it looks like he might still be counting bats in his head. I watch his face for interpretation and begin to understand that we are in a general state of distress. Hussein yells louder at the strange men and points at one of them and orders the chai boy out. Hameed does not speak. He has not taken out his notebook where he usually jots down notes during long stretches of conversation. He takes a half step closer to me and whispers, "They're mad."

I watch Hussein's face. His mustache is disturbed, and the left end of it points straight out, parallel with the ground, not down like it normally does. He points at me while yelling at the men. One of them takes a step toward me, points at the yellow folder, and yells at Hussein. Hameed takes another half step closer to me. "Is this about gun parts?" I ask him.

He stares at Hussein's gun, with its gold-embossed pistol grip, and says, "No."

A faint low buzz trickles into the room from somewhere in the hall, the sound of a tattoo machine gun or of incandescent lights slowly losing voltage. The chart on the TV disappears. The air conditioner stops. The lights flicker, as though concealed by a very large bat, and then go out. I hear one of the strange men shout louder at Hussein. Someone shuffles his feet across the floor. I open my eyes wider, trying to invent some light to penetrate the concrete blackness. When I strain hard enough, the darkness starts to move and form into other shapes, into the smashed grin of a small monkey, into the fanned tail of a white peacock. Hussein shouts back. A fist hits the table. Hameed moves closer to me and leans into my left side just behind me.

The sound of a pistol chambering a round is marked by a quick metallic grind as the slide moves rearward, and then a click as the round enters the chamber, and a louder click when the slide comes forward again. Each type of weapon has its own rhythm. On the larger weapons—.50 cals, 240s, MK-19 belt-fed grenade launchers, Barrett sniper rifles with lightweight bolt carriers—chambering a round can take the force of your whole body weight rocked into the charging handle. In a pistol, producing a grind and two consecutive clicks still takes a discernible amount of force, but it becomes easier with practice. In a windowless, powerless room at midnight, it is hard to distinguish the sound of four charging pistols in the hands of practiced men from a single pistol charging and echoing.

"Do something," Hameed whispers.

The yelling stops.

"*Wahed*," one of the strange men says.

"*Nen*," Hussein says back.

I know these words. They are counting. In America, we count to three before we hear what a swift grind, two clicks, and a trigger squeeze sounds like.

"*Thlata!*"

There is no sound but deep breaths.

"*Arba'a!*"

I wonder how high we must count in Arabic before someone, or all of us, is shot in this dark concrete box.

"*Khamsa!*"

Then the faint hum of a tattoo machine gun in the hallway behind us. The sound of television static. The chart reappears on the TV and the fan starts. The lights flicker back on.

Squinting now and blinking frequently, I see Hussein's pistol is pointed at the first strange man. The man to the right of the first stranger points his gun at Hameed, who is mostly hidden behind me and armed only with a green notebook and a pen in his back pocket. The other strange man points his pistol at Hussein. The first strange man points his pistol at me, and it is close enough that I could touch it by making the same motion I use to put on a hat or salute a higher-ranking officer. My pistol is in its hip holster.

When we all stop blinking, the men lower their pistols and reholster them. Hussein calls for chai and takes the yellow folder back. We look at the TV and stir our tea, and Hussein dismisses us. He smooths his mustache and says, "*Naqueeb Jameela*," softly while he hugs me on the way out.

Hameed and I get in the car and maneuver around the sleeping sheep.

"You didn't do anything," Hameed says. "You didn't even move a little."

Sheep sleep in the shadows of the trees in the parking lot, lit by a single bulb on the outside of the ITOC. I roll down a window, try to feel the outside air, and silently cry. "You're not supposed to cry," Hameed says, "you're supposed to do something."

9

The Omars

"IS IT ABOUT THE GENERATOR?" I ASK. HAMEED SHRUGS only his left shoulder and walks to the car. After weeks of not meeting with us, Hisham called Hammed and said he wants to see me. We arrive at Hisham's office and pass through the hall decorated with what appears to be everything one could buy at an Asian novelty store. There are screens painted with flowers, small Buddha statues, a ceramic panda, a Zen rock garden, a bronze elephant. A new porcelain doll with red lips, a white face, and black hair smiles at us while it stands next to the elephant. Hanging on the wall in Hisham's office are two brand-new tennis rackets—still plastic wrapped—arranged so they form the two slanted sides of an equilateral triangle. Underneath the plastic-wrapped tennis rackets is a large silver curved-blade sword with an ornate gold handle and red tassel. To the side of the tennis rackets is a clock with the silhouette of two soldiers whose hands tick time counterclockwise. On the facing wall are three mounted AK-47s, one with a magazine loaded. Hisham maintains a separate room to the right of his office where he keeps gifts and goes to pray at irregular intervals.

We sit down in our chairs, which flank a black marble table positioned in front of Hisham's large dark-cherry desk. On the table, carefully arranged in a triangle, are a whale-shaped blown-glass candy dish with chocolates wrapped in orange paper, a vase of pink and yellow plastic tulips, and a cocked revolver with Saddam's head engraved on the grip. The hammer is back.

Hisham enters the room and turns on the lights. We stand

up and shake hands, kiss cheeks, and place our right hands over our hearts.

"*A salaam alaikum, saydie, shlonick?*" I say.

"*Zeyn, zeyn, elhamdulillah, shlonich?*" he says back.

"*Zeyna, elhamdulillah,*" I say.

Hisham greets Hameed in a similar way, but they have more to say. Hisham extends his hands toward our chairs while he walks around to sit at his desk. "*Yalla,*" Hisham says and the door to his office opens. One of his soldiers in uniform comes in and stands to Hisham's right side, slightly behind where Hisham sits, in his blue jumpsuit, at his desk.

"This is Omar." Hameed jots notes down in Arabic on his green notebook while he interprets. "He is an excellent soldier. Very loyal. He is an electrician. His favorite color is pink, like this flower, and he works very hard."

"His favorite color is pink?" I ask.

"Pink is the strongest color," Hameed interprets. "It shows good taste and a brave heart. Omar would make a very good husband." Hameed looks at Hisham and then at me and smiles as he interprets. "What do you say?"

I look at Hameed, tilt my head a little to the side, and slightly narrow my eyes. This meeting is not about a generator. Hameed interprets, "Colonel Hisham would like to know if you think Omar would be a good husband for you."

I stare at Hameed hoping he'll tell me what to say, but he sits with his pen out, ready to take notes. I move my eyes around the room at random, trying to find a good answer here, but I see only a clock that tells time backward. After an uncomfortable silence, I say: "He's a fine man. But I don't think it is going to work."

Hameed interprets this to Hisham, whose eyes open widely. He presses his lips together, half smiling, nods, and takes out a blue Post-it–sized piece of paper. He writes on it, signs his name, stamps it with the unit's official stamp, and gives it to Omar, who thanks Hisham, bows toward him, then turns and bows to me before he walks to the door. He turns about to face Hisham again, salutes, and stomps his right foot. Hisham nods back and Omar leaves. Hisham stands up and shakes our hands, kisses our cheeks, and dismisses us.

"That's it?" I ask Hameed.

"At least he got a new pair of shoes out of it," Hameed says as we walk to the car. He explains that the blue paper was authorization for new boots.

"He got a new pair of boots for being a good potential husband?" I ask.

Hameed laughs and shrugs only his left shoulder.

IT'S BEEN FOUR DAYS SINCE HISHAM GAVE OMAR BOOTS AS a consolation for not marrying me, and Hameed comes to tell me that Hisham would like to see me again. Abbas, the unit sergeant major, meets us and leads us into Hisham's office. Standing next to Hisham is another soldier in uniform, whom I recognize from my haircut. We greet and before we sit down, Hisham says, "This is Omar. He is a commando who was wounded on a mission where he saved two Iraqis and an American. He can't be a commando anymore because of the injury, so he is the barber. He is very loyal and a very hard worker. His favorite color is also pink." Hameed snickers as he jots notes and interprets. "What do you say?"

I count the chocolate in the blowhole tray and after a deep breath say, "I think he seems like a fine and brave man." I look at Hisham, who half smiles. "But I don't think it will work."

Hisham takes a small blue piece of paper, writes on it, signs it, stamps it, and gives it to this Omar. Omar takes it, walks to the door, faces about, salutes and stomps his foot, and is dismissed. Hisham stands, shakes our hands, and dismisses us as well.

"Boots?" I ask Hameed as we walk to the car.

"A new warm-up suit," Hameed says. "The one with the capri pants that say 'Special Forces' down the side in gold letters."

Two days later Hameed summons me to Hisham's office again. By now I have read the advisory *Tactics Techniques and Procedures* cover to cover, and I did not find the section that discusses how to avoid marriage offers with Iraqi men. What I found on page after page is that relationships accomplish the mission (eventually) and that we must first build rapport and trust before we can expect action. So perhaps, indirectly, a marriage would mean I could talk about the generator that still sits uninstalled outside the compound. My American leadership questions why we don't just install the generator ourselves; we could. But one day we will leave, and if we continue to do everything for the Iraqis, as we have for the last decade, we will fail to help them realize self-sufficiency.

We walk into Hisham's building, where Abbas meets us and brings us into Hisham's office. We greet. Abbas brings tea. Hisham and Hameed talk about their families. Someone knocks on Hisham's door. "*Yalla*," Hisham says and a soldier in uniform pants but no shirt enters the room, marches to Hisham's right and slightly behind where he sits, and faces about to see us. I recognize him from the gym, where we tested cat treadmills and jiggle machines while he held a large weight and told us about the equipment's merits.

"This is Omar," Hisham says. "He is first place in Iraqi body building contest. He was a commando and killed many bad people before he was wounded. Now he runs the gym and lifts very heavy weight," Hameed interprets, shaking with inaudible laughter.

Hisham directs Omar to flex his muscles, turn around, and flex his back muscles. "His favorite color is pink and the gym is very neat. No one is allowed to wear shoes."

Hameed looks at me and waits, swallowing laughter in a way that bobs only his left shoulder.

"He looks very strong," I say. "But I don't think it's going to work."

Hisham dismisses Omar, who exits by saluting and stomping with no shirt on. Hameed and Hisham discuss something while I sit and wonder how many more men named Omar and whose favorite color is pink I will have to meet before we can talk about the generator.

"He wants to know what is wrong with Omar," Hameed says.

"Which Omar?"

"Any of them."

I stare at the Saddam-adorned pistol that sits cocked on the table in front of me, pointed at the tennis rackets on the wall, and ponder what exactly is wrong with the Omars I've been presented: they are men; they are Iraqi; they work for a unit that occasionally kills people in the middle of the night in their homes; they cannot leave the base because they will be killed by the general population of their own country; they work for a unit that will keep dead soldiers on their personnel documents so the commanders continue to get their paychecks—in U.S. dollars.

"The problem, *saydie*," I say and Hameed interprets, "is that my father cannot meet any of them. So no matter how brave, or strong, or fond of pink, they can't get my father's blessing."

Hisham gulps down a large breath of the perfumed air in his office, raises the corners of his mouth, and nods. He takes a blue sheet of paper, writes on it, signs it, stamps it, gives it to me, then dismisses us. "Boots or a tracksuit?" I ask as we walk to the car.

IT IS ALMOST RAMADAN, AND HISHAM NEEDS HELP SMUG-gling fifty cans of propane through a U.S. base, past the Ugandan guards, through the gate with no number, and onto our Iraqi base to make sure they have enough for *Eid*. Normally, Hisham's men can make this passage legally through one of the numbered gates because the propane runner, Omar (not the electrician, barber, or topless gym manager), is named in a letter that allows this to happen. But he is only allowed to bring in enough propane to cook the normal amount of food, and this time we need enough to adequately celebrate the end of Ramadan.

Hisham is the only one of my Iraqis who submits paperwork on time, which is why Omar can drive the propane in the first place. It took us two and a half months to get "Propane Omar" certified to transport propane in Iraq, sometimes through U.S.-occupied territory, because he has the same last name as another Omar who, as the intelligence agency tells us, is the brother of the Butcher of Balad: a "nefarious contact." Each time I submitted the approval letter to command, they returned it stating that he is a known terrorist and that if I know his whereabouts, I should consider turning him over to U.S. troops.

Hameed and I return to Hisham's office to see what we can do about the propane.

"*Saydie*," I say to Hisham from my seat adjacent to the loaded Saddam pistol, "the intelligence people tell us Propane Omar's brother is a known bad person."

Hameed interprets. Hisham pushes his chair away from his desk, walks to the window, opens it, and leans out dialing two cell phones. One of them connects, and he has a loud conversation with the other end. When he finishes, he sits back down. Hameed interprets, "Omar is on his way. You can ask him."

After two rounds of chai, Omar arrives and is made to stand motionless, staring at the loaded AK-47 to the right of Hisham's desk.

"How many people have you killed?" Hisham asks Omar.

"*Sufir! Sufir!*" he says—zero. Then Hameed interprets that he is a baker and doesn't even shoot guns, and unlike so many of his countrymen, he doesn't even like them.

"How many people has your brother killed?"

Omar moves, lowers his head, and answers so softly that Hameed has to lean toward him. When Omar finishes, he returns to his original position.

"He says his brother died in 2005 when he was shot on his way to university. Maybe by an Iraqi. Maybe by an American."

"See," Hisham says, and Hameed interprets, "How can his brother be bad if he is dead?" Hisham takes a square of blue paper, jots something down, stamps it, and hands it to Omar before he is dismissed.

I TELL THE ARMY INTELLIGENCE OFFICER THAT I HAVE SPO-
ken with Omar and learned that his brother has been dead for
six years.

"You should consider turning him over to U.S. troops," he
advises, "since you seem to know his whereabouts."

I tell this to Montana, who vets the four thousand Iraqi sol-
diers we live with—a process done independently because, as
Montana told me the first week I was here, we understand the
Iraqis differently than the regular army does.

"It's because there are twelve Omars with his last name," Montana tells me. "Big Army just can't figure out a way to sort them
out, so they just assume they are all bad. I guess it's safer," he says
as he dons his Kevlar vest, puts a jacket over it, and climbs into
an unmarked blue up-armored Trailblazer on his way to meet
with some of his sources. It is this elaborate network of sources
that helped us acquire an antenna for the Armed Forces Network
and the amplifier that lets us get the signal from the nearest U.S.
base. It is this elaborate network of sources that lets us track and
follow certain targets we believe to have hostile intentions. It is
because of this elaborate network of sources that we know about
major indirect fire attacks ahead of time and usually avoid them.
It is this elaborate network of sources that brings us watermelon
from farms outside of Baghdad when they are in season. It is this
elaborate network of sources that provides a constant supply of
Tennessee bourbon to our compound and alerts us to changes
in certain networks of Iranian-backed militias to the south. And
it is because we have such an elaborate network of sources that
we know Propane Omar is not related to the Butcher of Balad,
or any other nefarious contacts.

But like so much of what we do here, we don't share this network because it has taken more than a decade to develop and
because we can't trust anyone else with it. The regular army's
allegiance to good order and discipline and General Order 1B—
the directive that prohibits alcohol, civilian clothing, and sex—

has no room for watermelon, crisp bourbon, reappropriated TV antennae, and real-time intelligence.

Now that our Propane Omar is back on their watch list, as are the other eleven Omars in Iraq with his family name—one of whom is related to the Butcher of Balad—Hisham calls me to his office to ask me how we will get enough propane for Ramadan.

"*Saydie*," I say, and Hameed interprets, "give me four days and I will have a solution."

"Ramadan begins in three days," he says. Hameed interprets distress.

"*Nam, saydie*," I say, "you will have enough propane. I need to see Omar."

Hisham's eyes widen. "Which Omar?"

"Propane Omar," I say as Hameed laughs silently, raising only his left shoulder.

We get up and drive with Hisham to the bakery where Omar works.

We eat *samoon* with Omar. He offers us freshly salted fish, and I watch as Hameed puts some on his bread, sweeps for pin bones with a swift pass of his index finger, and eats. I do the same and watch Hisham and Omar smile as I chew. We set our propane plan with Omar and before we leave, he asks if he may also bring a television set in with the propane. I say no problem and he hands me a blue square of paper with the TV's information, Hisham's official stamp, and his badge number. I put it in the pocket of my uniform and finish my chai.

The next day, Hameed and I meet Omar at an unmarked location in Montana's blue up-armored Trailblazer. We have words we must pass to certain people behind a wall, a key we must throw under a gate, and a certain direction we're not to look toward. We collect the key and Omar's large white canvas-covered trucks carrying 150 bottles of propane, a 37-inch Panasonic flat-screen television, and an unannounced blue duffle bag that I don't ask about. Along the way back to our compound, we pass a U.S. convoy of MRAPs that swivel their remote-controlled gun turrets our way as they assess us as a threat. Our windows are tinted, almost opaque, but our license plate says we are friendly, so the gun swivels away from us and pauses on Omar's truck. It stays there until the MRAPs exit and head back to Camp Victory. Omar and his shipment make it safely back to base. Before we leave him, he passes along a gold-plated Dragunov sniper rifle as a gift for our help. I give it to Aaron as a thank you for finally letting me cut a car in half with the mini. He cannot understand why I don't want it and, for the next month, keeps asking where I got it.

"From a source," I say.

HAMEED KNOCKS ON MY DOOR. IT IS ALMOST 1:00 A.M.

"Hisham needs to see you right away," Hameed tells me and waves his cell phone by his head. I change out of my polar bear–patterned pajamas, arm, and drive with Hameed over to Hisham's office. It is dark when we arrive, except for a newly added orange lava lamp that sits between a bronze woolly mammoth statue and the fountain at the entryway. We knock at the door. Hisham shines the flashlight from one of his cell phones at us and marshals us in. Before we greet, Hisham begins to speak.

"I am sorry for calling so late," Hameed interprets. "But I am leaving right now for Ramadan leave."

He pauses. Hameed says, "*Ramadan kareem, saydie.*"

Hisham turns on the blue and orange stained-glass lamp on his desk. He bows toward Hameed and echoes the greeting.

"*Ramadan kareem, saydie,*" I say. He bows in my direction.

"He wasn't sure if you would be gone after Ramadan, so he needed to see you tonight," Hameed says.

Hisham takes a large garbage bag off the floor and sets it on his desk. He stands, a towering presence behind the desk in the soft lamplight. Hameed interprets as Hisham gives the longest uninterrupted soliloquy I have ever heard him speak.

"He is, of course, still worried you don't have a husband," Hameed begins, speaking to me while he listens to Hisham and jots notes down in his small green notebook. "He asked Omar to help him with this, and Omar was able to bring some of these things in with the propane, which he thanks you for getting. You are the best adviser so far, you ask only questions that help, and you actually do what you say. He has made—" Hameed stops, raises his hand, and discusses something with Hisham.

"He has made a kit for you. It will help you find a husband as soon as you get home. He thinks your father will like it." I look at Hameed, but he is too busy navigating two conversations about an unfamiliar matter to speak to me with his left shoulder.

Hisham, as his way of expressing gratitude for moving propane; acquiring speed bumps, a generator, and a Reverse Osmosis Water Purification Unit (that they don't use); and sharing fresh *samoon* has, with one of the Omars, assembled my husband kit.

Hameed explains each item as it emerges from the black trash bag. First, a handmade burgundy dishdasha, hand embroidered with gold thread. It looks like a bohemian hippie dress, with flaring three-quarter-length sleeves and a square neckline. His wife decided on the color and had their tailor in Diyala make it just for me.

"So your husband will look at you and your clothing will be as beautiful as you," Hameed explains.

Next, a pair of size-eight turquoise heels with large flowers on the tops. "The natural complement to the dishdasha."

I nod.

Then two pairs of stockings. One set of fishnets in the style that hooks to the kind of underwear people get at bachelorette parties—which are not in the garbage bag—and the other patterned with butterflies, "for modesty."

Next, a purple Versace scarf. We pause to practice wrapping my head with it, which my time with Mara has taught me to do well, then receive instructions to grow my hair longer so it can be seen from the back, "for mystery."

Then a tea set with twelve cups, plates, and miniature spoons adorned with date palms and the outline of Iraq, "for entertaining."

Hameed explains that it is not enough to simply have the tea set, I must know how to use it; hence, the tea kettle and four bags of traditional Iraqi chai, brewed with cardamom. Then the Turkish coffee pot, which looks most like a genie lamp, made entirely of polished brass and covered in a pattern similar to expensive Persian rugs and the ceiling of the Alhambra. "Jody will tell you how to brew the tea and how to pour it," Hisham tells me. Jody does, in fact, make the best chai I've had here.

Next, four Ziploc bags with Arabic words scrawled in green marker across the front. "These are spices for cooking—he wants to make sure you cook," Hameed says. "I told him of course you do, but he needs to hear you say you cook. Even if you don't just say yes."

"*Nam, saydie, nam,*" I say.

Hisham nods and continues. "This one is a bag of cardamom seeds. This one is sumac, which is very expensive in the U.S. This one is for boiled meat," Hameed says as he points to a baggie that is half full of brown powder and half full of yellow powder.

"So what is it?" I ask.

"For boiled meat," Hameed says as he moves his finger across the green writing on the bag. "And this one," pointing to a bag of half white powder and half gray powder, "is for grilled meat."

Then a set of amber worry beads for my future husband, "for luck, and as a demonstration of social status." Hisham is the only person I've seen with an amber set.

Last, Hisham takes out two watermelons, "because he likes watermelon." He cuts into one, and we eat fresh watermelon in his office by lamplight as he puts the contents of my husband kit back in the bag. So certain is he that a burgundy dishdasha, turquoise heels, a purple head scarf, two pairs of stockings, a tea set, a tea kettle, a Turkish coffee pot, four bags of tea, four bags of mixed spices, and amber worry beads will find me a husband, he says, "Congratulations on your engagement. Tell your father that Omar and I wish him well."

By the lava lamp in the entryway, we bow and exchange *Ramadan kareems* again. "*Shukran, saydie. Shukran,*" I say again. He nods, clicks off the lava lamp, and watches until the lava falls and starts to congeal. Hameed laughs, shrugging only his left shoulder, when we get in the car. "Better than a tracksuit," he says and holds the watermelon as we drive away into the night, passing the dining hall, dark except for the blue-orange glow of two propane burners in the back near the bakery.

10

History Lessons

HAMEED SAYS THAT THE DUST STORMS WERE NEVER THIS bad before he left Iraq for a woman in Wisconsin. His theory is that during the war, tanks and helicopters churned up the dust in the desert and now there is a lot more loose dust that gets picked up and blown by the wind.

"Which war?" I ask him.

"Both," he says. "And since MRAPs weigh so much, there is even more loose dust now."

We're standing on the roof of Building Five, another of Saddam's ornate old government buildings. I look at the Tigris and think about tanks and MRAPs and helicopters loosening up dirt that had been in place since Gilgamesh.

"You know what I think America's problem is?" Hameed asks me.

"We make vehicles too heavy for most of the bridges in the world," I say.

He stands near the railing of this roof and looks out over the Tigris and watches the flat, thick grassy leaves blow in the wind along its banks.

"And I love Americans," he says, "but we think we are immune to history."

Schwab walks over to us and looks across the river. The three of us wander around the roof of this building, finding a bunker, a machine gun, and a stack of golf clubs, two buckets of range balls, and a net into which we hit some balls, nine stories up in Baghdad. Schwab and I try to hit a ball beyond the perimeter wall with a 4-iron. I get much closer than he does. I try to offer some pointers on coordinating his hip rotation with his arm swing, but he's uninterested and throws the club into the net before we go back down the stairs to find Miller and get some coffee.

The meeting that brought us here was only an hour long, and we have some time to kill before our convoy is supposed to leave again. We couldn't drive ourselves this time because Perry's guys didn't fix their gun trucks and, prioritizing the relative importance of their role (counterterrorism operations) versus ours (logistics), took our gun trucks. So instead, we drove ourselves in the plum Trailblazer to the air base and jumped into its convoy shuttle. I can't remember why we thought Miller should come with us, and I can't remember why he thought he should. I think it is because he heard they have avocados at the dining facility. I can't remember why Hameed needed to come either, since everyone we are meeting with speaks English, but I think he also heard about the avocados. At lunch, before the golf lesson, I ate the equivalent of five avocados on top of some spinach, called it a salad, and thought maybe I should bring some back with me in a to-go box. Until today, I hadn't had an avocado in close to a year.

We leave the coffee shop and go back to get our body armor and weapons and the three-hundred-page *Little Green Book* on security assistance management that I got as a guide from the meeting, and we go to the designated meeting point. We pass a navy O-3.

"Did you see her name?" I ask.

"Nope, didn't bother," says Schwab.

"That was Captain Downer," I say and think to myself, I hope she gets promoted to major soon.

"She's in the navy," Schwab says. "Wouldn't that make her a lieutenant or something?"

Major Downer.

There is a small gathering at the meeting point. People lean back against their body armor and shade their eyes from the sun. It occurs to me that none of these people have ammunition for their long rifles except for us. They don't even have ammunition holders in which to potentially carry any load, much less a full combat load. Somehow, in the eighth year of this war, it has become unnecessary for people to bring bullets with them. We require heavy, ill-fitting armor, helmets, ballistic eyewear, gloves, individual first aid kits. Most of these people have earplugs dangling off their body armor to dampen the noise of the shots they can't take, and none of them, it appears, have bothered to remove their Combat Action Tourniquets from their plastic packaging. Back in New Jersey, where the avocado drought first started, we went through Combat Lifesaver, taught by a combat medic with seven tours in Afghanistan. We spent three days learning how to apply a tourniquet to ourselves and each other. During a lunch break, while *Restrepo* played on the projection screen, the medic instructor kicked the door to the classroom open, shut off the lights, yelled, "TOURNIQUET—LEFT ARM!" and shot off a clip of blanks. He turned the lights back on to see who could not apply a tourniquet in the amount of time it took to fire thirty blank rounds on burst. He then came to check everyone's self-application to determine whether we would have lived, generally judged by how cold and blue our hands were turning and if he could feel a radial pulse. "There are two certain ways to die," he told us. "If you run out of ammunition, and if you don't take the tourniquet out of the package now."

One of the people reclining on their bulletless armor wonders if there is a problem with the shuttle.

"I take this all the time," the reclining man says, "and they are never late."

We wait a little longer. He gets out his cell phone and calls someone from his office. "Yes," he says to the phone, "just read me what it says on the screen. No, the secret screen. Oh. I think. Canceled until Monday? It's Thursday."

We get up and try to find a phone, preferably a secure one so when we ask someone to read secret information it will not be broadcasted over the Baghdad cellular waves.

"The chaplain," Hameed says.

"What about him?" Miller asks.

"He has a secret phone," says Hameed.

"Why do you know that?" Schwab asks. Hameed shrugs only his left shoulder and leaves to find us a place to stay.

In a small hallway in the chapel, standing next to a bowl of holy water and a crucifix of a historically accurate brown Jesus leaned up against the wall, Schwab dials up Perry's guys in the operations center. Next to the listing Jesus is a stack of pamphlets: *The New Testament and You*, *Loving Your Child Long Distance*, *Reintegrating with Your Pet*, a trifold on programs enlisted members can get to commission, a brief history of military rank. Thumbing through the heritage of military ranks, I learn enlisted navy members don't have ranks, they have rates. The Continental Army had the rank of subaltern, denoted by green cockades in their hats, which was any officer junior to captain. This rank was replaced by second lieutenant in 1800 but didn't get a separate insignia until 1917, when it earned the single gold bar. The navy equivalent, ensign, a rank that originated in the army as the person who carried the unit flag into battle, didn't receive its gold bar insignia until 1922. Until 1857, the navy, in its pursuit of clarity, had three ranks of captain, in addition to anyone commanding a ship also receiving the title, regardless of rank. During the Civil War, they had commodores.

"Until Monday," Schwab says to the secret phone. "For another Day of Rage. Can you come get us? No, well, how about a helicopter? Yes," he says, "do that. We will call back in an hour."

Schwab hangs up the phone. Miller is trying to see if the rim of the holy water bowl will ring like a crystal wine glass. Staring at Miller, the chaplain gives us the code to his door so if we need to come back and use the secret phone, we can get in. If we need confession, he advises, we need to schedule it in advance. I take the pamphlet with me.

Schwab, Miller, and I go to meet Hameed, who has already checked us into billeting, which is an odd building, perhaps originally a school, converted into a hotel. We head for our rooms and agree to meet back in twenty minutes to walk to the shoppette for toothpaste and socks. I'm in the "Female Wing." At the end of the hall in the Female Wing is a large bathroom with no door. Inside the room, to the left of the door, is a platform with a large bathtub. The shower curtain, which is screwed into the walls of the platform, has been pulled back. Visible to the right are a few more shower stalls. It appears most people wash their hands with the faucet of the large platformed bathtub. When I find my room number, I let myself into a large room (fourth grade science, perhaps) and put down my armor and rifle next to one of three empty beds, and I make the bed with the mismatched assortment of sheets they gave us.

To my delight, Captain Downer is my roommate. I see her body armor next to another colorfully made bed. I hope her name is Debbie. There are large filing cabinets in which we can store our weapons. Part of the bedding package is a padlock with the combination written on the bottom. We are told to secure our weapons in the cabinets with these locks, so I find one that is not currently in use, and I secure my weapon and the full combat load I have on my armor. Twenty minutes is a long time to make a bed, so I inspect the bathroom further. One of the double doors is missing, so the first shower stall is in direct sight of the hallway, which happens to contain not only my room but, a bit farther away, the front desk as well. Schwab, Hameed, and Miller are already at the front desk again, which I clearly see from the bathroom, so I meet them.

We walk to the other end of the base, which is not far, and find the shop. They have no shorts or shirts, but I buy the travel kit with toothpaste, shampoo, lotion, and a toothbrush and a pair of 89-cent flip-flops. I agree to share a six pack of socks with Miller if he buys me a Diet Dr. Pepper, which I forgot to buy when I checked out. I spend $7.35. Miller spends a little over $30. I lean against the large perimeter wall and wait for him to check out. The Days of Rage have been protests across Iraq, people gathering in Tahrir Square in demonstration against their country's corruption, bad public services, unemployment. Earlier this year, somewhere between a hundred thousand and five hundred thousand people, organized by Muqtada al-Sadr, took to Tahrir Square to protest the U.S. occupation of their country. Tahrir Square is across the Tigris from us, probably visible from the roof if we had bothered to look. In the center of it is the Freedom Monument, a series of black metal figures in motion, almost gymnastic, with a man in the center in a lunge, arms spread apart, breaking down prison bars. It was erected in 1961, celebrating the establishment of the Republic of Iraq, and each gymnastic metal sculpture represents a key event leading up to the republic's creation. I have seen renderings of this, elsewhere in Iraq, painted onto concrete t-walls leading to U.S.-held compounds, but those renderings, even the best ones, are cartoonish mimics of the real thing.

I only bought half a pack of socks and toiletries because I did bring an extra shirt but thought before I left that I wouldn't need more than that on the up-armored shuttle convoy here. The four of us walk back, drop off our things, and go back to the chapel to use the secret phone. Schwab calls the people who wouldn't fix their gun trucks and confirms that we can try to get on a helicopter, but they have little confidence in us doing so. Schwab calls a shuttle service to the helipad that comes in what looks like a dog-catcher van—three small porthole windows on each side, trapezoidal body shape, two rows of back tires. They will meet us at 8:45 p.m. I have avocados and tea cookies for dinner, and we go to the basement of Building Five, where there are computers and internet and TVs to pass the time.

When the time comes, we leave, go back to billeting, unmake the beds, open the filing cabinets housing our weapons and gear, turn in our sheets, and put all our things back on.

"We are going to try and fly out," I tell the desk attendant. "But can you hold our keys until about eleven in case we don't make it?"

She agrees, familiar with the situation. We walk to the volleyball court to meet the dogcatcher van. On the way, we let ourselves into the chapel so Schwab can call one more time.

"Weather canceled," he says.

Miller is outside eating meat sticks he finds in care packages to troops that have been left in the chapel. Hameed is drinking water. We walk to the volleyball courts and tell the dogcatchers that we don't need a ride anymore, and we walk back to the hotel. We agree to meet for lunch and call our people again tomorrow. I remake the bed with new sheets, lock my things in the cabinet with a different combo lock with the combo written on it, then select the bathtub stall for a shower because it is the only one that has a curtain. I get out my travel-sized Finesse, wash my hair, use my underwear as a luffa, and give it an extra Finesse wash. The bra has one more day before it gets a similar treatment. I put on my spandex shorts and the extra T-shirt and lie down in bed. I am reading Gayatri Chakravorty Spivak's "Can the Subaltern Speak," from my copy of *Marxism and the Interpretation of Culture*. The book is far too large to be practically carried around, and deciding to bring it meant I didn't bring extra socks. It's twice the length of the *Little Green Book* but has a red cover. Debbie walks into the room.

"Oh," she says when she sees me.

"Hi," I say and put down the book.

"I'm not a lesbian," she says.

"What?" I ask.

"Well, I just want you to know," she says.

"I wasn't worried," I say.

"I am," she says, ducks behind her filing cabinet, changes into workout clothes, and leaves. I fall asleep with all the lights on and use a sock as an eye mask.

THEY DO NOT HAVE AVOCADOS ON THE SECOND DAY, BUT the lemon poppy seed dressing is very good. We let ourselves into the chapel again. Miller rummages around for more preserved American treats.

"Tonight," Schwab says. "Are we manifested? But there are twelve open seats? Okay, we'll try again."

He calls the dogcatchers and arranges a pickup for 10:00 p.m. We head back to the basement to pass the time. Schwab shops for jewelry for his wife while I check ESPN.com. We eat the free overcooked popcorn. We get more coffee. We have an avocado-less dinner. Finally it is time. We check out and again ask that they hold our keys until midnight and walk to the volleyball courts. Access to the embassy compound has been a challenge, we're told, and we are not sure they will let us on. We board the dog-catcher van, where it is hot and the porthole windows are nause-ating. Miller hands me some water as we drive into the darkness. When we arrive, someone opens the door.

"I think all the flights are weather canceled," the man who opened the door says.

"We might as well check the terminal," Schwab says. "We're here."

I want out of the dogcatcher van. We get to the embassy com-pound. Someone new opens the door.

"Flights are on weather hold," the new man says.

"We should have probably engaged the combat locks on the van," Miller says to Hameed.

"We'll wait," Schwab says to the new man.

I want out of the dogcatcher van.

We give our IDs to the guy at the checkpoint and get out of the van and ask them to wait until we know if we are allowed in and if there will be a helicopter tonight.

"You are not on the list," the man says. "Did you email us?"

"No," I say, "we don't have a computer."

"Well, you need to request access two days in advance," he tells us.

"We didn't know that we would need access two days ago," I say.

"We're special forces," Miller says to the man, who looks at him, at me, at Hameed, at Schwab and assesses that there is nothing special forces about Miller's affinity for packaged meat sticks, or my gender, but Schwab and Hameed seem plausible.

A man in all khaki appears.

"Going to BIAP?" he asks.

"Close enough," I say.

"They're with me," he tells the man at the checkpoint, and he escorts us in and tells the dogcatcher to drive away. He brings us to the ambassador's lounge.

"All army birds are canceled tonight because of dust," he tells us.

"You just told our van to leave," Schwab says. I would rather sleep in the ambassador's lounge than get back in the dogcatcher van and spend another illuminated night with Major Downer.

"Get on the scales," khaki says.

We are weighed for weight and balance purposes on the aircraft. He offers us coffee. "When the birds land," he says, "wait with me. If you walk to them before the DV gets into his convoy, they will shoot you. Does everyone have earplugs?"

"Yes," we say.

"I'll come get you when it is time," he says. We sit in the lounge and note every fitness magazine ever printed has at least one article on belly fat and how it may be eliminated. Hameed slides them toward Miller one by one. Khaki points at us. We don our armor and earplugs and follow him, with sunglasses on in the middle of the night, outside onto a completely dark concrete pad surrounded on all sides by twelve-foot concrete walls. The light from the lounge is the only thing backlighting the darkness. The DV enters his convoy. Khaki hands me a box.

"Give this to Margaret," he tells me and points Hameed and me to the first helicopter. There are no lights on the pad. There are no lights on the bird. The light from the lounge has been turned off. I sit down, put on my seatbelt, and hold Margaret's box.

Baghdad looks different at night and from the air. It could be LA, or Kansas City, or Bakersfield, California. House lights flicker underneath us. Palm trees dance a little in the wind, backlit against streetlights lining residential streets. Maybe this is what it is like taking an aerial tour of Las Vegas. We pop flares before we fly over the airport. This is not Las Vegas. Hameed thinks we are getting shot at and motions for me to point my gun out the open door. The crew chief raises his night vision goggles and looks at him. The second bird pops flares too. Later we learn Miller also thought we were being shot at. We come in to land but remain in a low hover without touching down, landing lights on this time, and we wait for the crew chief to tell us to get off. A line of people waiting to load a C-130 with his engines running stare at us as we hop out of the ambassador's helicopters and walk toward the passenger terminal with Margaret's box.

The personnel specialist who lets us in the door there tries to make us sign in to the base.

"We never signed out," I tell her. "I doubt we're on your personnel tracker."

"Yes, you are," she says. "You have to be. We have to have a record of you being here."

Schwab has left us to find a phone to call Perry's guys for a ride.

"You can't go until we update your status," the personnel specialist tells us.

"I don't think you'll be able to do that," I tell her.

She searches for us in her system. "There is no history for you in here," she says, clicking vigorously between screens and spreadsheet rows. Schwab comes back to tell us they will be here in a half hour or so. Miller is eating some cookies left on the table. The personnel specialist tries Miller's name, which they find, but it's the wrong Miller, and the one in their database redeployed last month. She searches for Schwab and finds nothing, not even an initial entry for our team months ago. She asks for Hameed's information. He laughs. She goes to find her supervisor, and they return together.

"They have no history," she says, clicking and pointing.

"Where did you come from?" the supervisor asks.

"The embassy," I say.

"There were no flights out of there today," the supervisor says.

"Maybe that's why they were out of avocados," Miller says.

"You can't have come from there," the supervisor says.

"Where would you like us to have come from?" I ask.

Hameed leaves to wait for the van out front with Schwab.

The personnelist and her supervisor continue clicking, pointing, searching for our history. Miller eats the rest of the cookies. Schwab opens the door and waves at us to follow him.

"This is for Margaret," I tell the personnelist and leave the box on the table.

"Who's Margaret?" she asks.

I don't know. We jump into the van, which has no sliding side door. Aaron is driving and one of his team guys sits in the front seat with a 240B.

"Who do you know that got you on the ambassador's fleet?" Aaron asks us. No one knows khaki's name or who he was. Aaron waits for a reply.

"Margaret," I say as we drive out the gate of the base that has no history of us, out the t-walled perimeter of the U.S.-controlled area. One of the last t-wall sections we pass has a single painted t-wall with a man in a lunge, arms outstretched, cropped at the elbows, missing the rest of his mural.

11

The Kill List

"POWER'S OUT," SCHWAB SAYS FROM WHERE HE SITS WITH Francis and Hameed. "Oh, and Hameed told me one of the GSU guys died today."

I look at Hameed, who is fanning himself with his small green notebook in his right hand. He shrugs his left shoulder and keeps fanning.

"Someone died, Hameed?"

"Yeah, it was Ali the electrician. He was trying to fix a light in the dining hall Hisham told him had to be fixed before he could eat there again. Guess he forgot to cut off the power."

"He was electrocuted in the dining hall?"

"No, someone knocked him off the ladder before he got all the way electrocuted. He fell on his head. Hisham said he died from that."

"You talked to Hisham?"

"Yeah, he says he needs more propane."

Just back from a meeting with Jade's team, I sit down, between Schwab and Hameed, on one of the u-shaped benches on the small wooden camouflage net–covered gazebo. Francis, Schwab's interpreter, moves a little farther away from me. Unlike Hameed, who claims Bakersfield, California, as home, Francis is a local national, born in Baghdad, and he hasn't been able to escape. Our local national interpreters all selected American names. Brad, one of our former interpreters—who was a chemical engineer before he learned he could make better money translating vehicle maintenance manuals for the U.S. government—chose his name because he wanted people to confuse him with Brad Pitt, though Brad Pitt is nearly a half foot taller, blond, and American. Francis won't tell us why he chose Francis as his American name, and he won't tell us his real name either. When we ask him about it, he moves his stiff black baseball cap by the bill, left and right, and strokes his mustache. He will not sit next to me (out of respect, he says) and prefers to be at least an arm's length away at all times. When I ask him if he could explain the roots of this custom to me, he adjusts his ball cap and mustache.

I lean back on the bench and Francis moves closer to the end before he gets up, turns to Schwab, and says, "We must prepare for the *fatiha*." Then he brushes off his hands on his pants and walks away.

"So how was the meeting?" Schwab asks me.

"What's a *fatiha*?" I ask Hameed.

Hameed looks at the seat where Francis sat, still marked by the sweat print we all leave when sitting outside in 120-degree heat. "Hisham says the *fatiha* is tonight at seven," Hameed says. He and Francis have both been working here for five or six years. "We should go."

The *fatiha* is the first of the Quran's 114 chapters. It has seven verses and is recited before all other prayers. Hameed tells me that Muslims who follow traditional rules recite it seventeen times a day. It is a prayer for guidance and is said at the beginning and the end of each night during the three-day mourning ceremony, also called a *fatiha*, when someone dies. Hameed explains that everyone sits around in a circle and says the *fatiha*, and then we have tea or coffee while someone else reads other parts of the Quran, and then we thank the host and leave. We do this twice, and on the third night, we also have a large feast.

"What if you don't know the *fatiha*?" I ask Hameed.

"You should learn it," Hameed says.

"Do I have to go to this thing?" Schwab asks me.

"Yes," I say, though I have no reason to make him go.

"You should learn the *fatiha*," Hameed says.

144

"Right," Schwab says, stands up, and walks away to sit in different shade.

I ask Hameed to teach me the *fatiha*.

Bismi Allah al-rahman al-raheem
Elhamdulallah i rabbil 'alameen.
Ar-Rahman ar-Raheem Maaliki yaumid Deen.
Iyyaaka na'abudu wa iyyaaka nasta'een
Ihdinas siraatal mustaqeem
Siraatal ladheena an 'amta' alaihim
Ghairil maghduubi' alaihim waladaaleen
Ameen.

We practice it. I cannot pronounce the last two verses. He tries writing down the last two verses phonetically, but his understanding of phonetics and mine are as different as the schools in Baghdad and Albuquerque where each of us first learned them.

"What does it mean?" I ask him.

"That won't help you say it," he says.

We hear the generator fire up again and air conditioners start across our compound. I look at the clock next to the whiteboard where Hameed has written "gkh-ar-il" in explanation. The digital thermometer on this clock reached 135 degrees one day and then melted. The screen has been permanently black and pixilated ever since. The clock still works, except that it cannot properly display the middle horizontal bar that distinguishes an eight from a zero.

"I have a meeting with Perry," I say.

"Let's meet at 6:45. We'll drive over to Hisham's building together for the *fatiha*. Keep practicing," Hameed says and walks away.

ON PERRY'S SIDE OF THE COMPOUND—THE SIDE WHERE his Green Beret teams live, the side with a gym and indoor plumbing, the side that doesn't lose power in the middle of the day—I arrive late to the 5:00 p.m. meeting (it was actually 4:58 when I left, not 4:50), which has started without me. I sit on the wooden bench near the back wall by the large steel door. Perry looks at me and nods.

"We'll have to kill Osman," Jordan says. "He's a really good shot."

Jordan sits around the large table in the operations center with the rest of the members of his team, which for the last eight years has been responsible for training the sniper company of the Iraqi Special Operations Forces we now live and work with. Next to him, Travis packs a Tootsie Roll–sized dip in his front lip and scratches his head with a nibbled yellow Ticonderoga pencil. We were supposed to be an enduring presence here, staying even after the main U.S. force withdrawal in December, but we found out a few hours ago that has changed and we too are leaving, packing up and driving out of this place to stage somewhere else and wait to be called back in. I'm here because I'm responsible for logistics, both the Iraqis' and our own. Someone, fearing we will have nothing to eat when the road we take to the nearest U.S. base for lunch becomes too dangerous to drive (in two to five weeks, estimated) has ordered forty-five thousand Meals Ready to Eat without a concept of how much space seventy-five pallets of food that never expires requires for storage, or where we might put them so they are not all immediately stolen by our Iraqi counterparts.

Perry asked me to come. He said it was urgent that I am a part of the drawdown plan, and as he is my boss and a Green Beret on his ninth deployment, I do what he says. But this meeting is not about MREs, or the sixty pallets of water we need to order before the Water Purification Plant closes next month. It is about identifying which of the Iraqis Jordan and his guys have trained we need to kill before we leave to reduce the threat of resistance in the event we reinvade their country in the future.

"What about Khalid?" Travis asks.

"No, Khalid is fine. He couldn't hit the spinning metal target from the 150-meter tower with the good scope," Jordan says.

"Ali?"

"Which one?"

"Ali the sniper. He seems as good as Osman. Remember what he did in Amman?"

"Yeah, Ali too. But Ali the spotter is cool. He's not very good."

Jordan jots down Ali the sniper's name on his yellow legal pad next to Osman's name and a sketch of a cartoonish cowboy being flung off a rearing bronco with an enormous erection.

"Anyone else?" Perry asks.

"I can't think of anyone else from Second Battalion," Jordan says.

"What about First Battalion?" Perry asks Brandon, First Battalion's primary adviser.

"Maybe only Akhil," Brandon says. Jordan adds Akhil's name to the list.

"What about you?" Perry asks me.

I work with the soldiers, bakers, mechanics, and electricians who run the bakery, the anti-hijacking unit, the hospital, the dining halls, the prime minister's personal security detail, a heavy equipment company, and some guys who drive and fix a ten-ton crane.

"What?" I say as I watch Jordan sketch a six-shooter into the cowboy's hand.

"Anyone you work with that we need to eliminate before we leave?"

"Do you know who ordered the MREs?" I ask.

"What about Bakr?" Perry asks Matt.

Matt finishes packing a dip into his lip and looks up at Perry. "Eh," he says, "could go either way. Hey, Jordan, I forgot to sign up for the 1911, can I still get in on that?"

Behind Perry's chair hangs a whiteboard on the wall on which Jordan has started taking orders for fancy pistols with their battalion shield etched into the grip. They offered me the chance to order one. Jordan writes Matt's name down on his paper on the other side of the horse, opposite Osman, Khalid, and Ali the sniper's names.

"One of Hisham's soldiers died today," I say.

"Are you sure you don't want one?" Jordan asks and leans back in his chair. He says, "Once in a lifetime."

"Be a nice present for your boyfriend," Matt says and grins.

The meeting ends and Travis and Matt leave to find more Grizzly. Jordan stays behind to talk to me about the merits of the 1911 pistol, about how he likes his Glock just fine, but if you're buying a pistol, and you should be, the 1911 is the best way to go. Then he says this is the first he's heard about a boyfriend and asks me questions about him. I catch Perry as he stands up to leave.

"I won't be at the ops and intel meeting tonight," I say. "One of Hisham's soldiers died and I'm going to his *fatiha*."

"Well, shit," Perry says.

FRANCIS SITS IN THE SAME PLACE AS ALWAYS ON THE wooden bench and waits for us to go to the *fatiha*. He sits under the melted digital thermometer, holding the edges of the bench, and rocks back and forth. Schwab and Hameed aren't here yet. The clock says 6:40 (or 6:48).

After enough time passes to see that it is now 6:41, Francis says "I hate Iraqis" and leans back, shifts his black ball cap side to side, and strokes his mustache.

"You hate Iraqis?" I ask him.

"Yes," he says and bobs his head as though he has the hiccups, "these motherfuckers have ruined their country." He points his index finger to the sky.

"Isn't it your country too?" I ask him.

"Mine," he says, "is not a country of crazy motherfuckers."

Hameed and Schwab arrive in time to hear this and both look at me. I start walking toward the door of our compound, and Schwab, Hameed, and Francis follow me. Francis hates that I drive and has told Schwab this many times in private conversations they have under the melted clock. Schwab has since managed to give his car to someone else and now rides almost everywhere with me. He gets into the front seat, and Francis and Hameed get in the back. Francis rides with his arms crossed over his chest the whole time staring out the window.

I change the channel from Hayati FM to the Armed Forces Network radio station in time to catch the last half of a Lady Gaga song. Schwab turns up the volume.

"It is disrespect to listen to music on the way to a *fatiha!*" Francis shouts from the back seat. Schwab turns the music up louder.

We park in front of Hisham's building, turn down the music, and go to join a circle of once-white plastic chairs that are now brittle on their surface like unfired clay. We greet Hisham, who is somber but glad to see me.

"*Asalaam aleykum, saydie, schlonick?*" I say, shake Hisham's hand, and place my right hand over my heart as we bow to each other.

"*Zen, elhamdulallah, schlonich?*" he says.

"*Zeyna, zeyna, elhamdulallah,*" I say back. Hameed and Francis greet him the same way, but with more to say. Schwab shakes his hand and nods in silence.

"You don't say all the syllables right in *elhamdulallah,*" Francis says to me as we walk toward Abu Najeeb, Ali the electrician's closest friend and our host.

"*Maku mushkala,*" I say back.

Abu Najeeb shakes our hands. Hameed interprets that he is honored we came. We shake the hands of all the other soldiers, bakers, mechanics, and electricians gathered in the horseshoe of brittle white plastic chairs. It is the first time I have met most of them, and their handshakes are long as they look at me.

We sit down near the end in order, Francis, Schwab, me, then Hameed, as we watch the rest of the people arriving do the same ritual of handshakes. When most people are seated, everyone turns their palms to the sky, on their knees, closes their eyes, and begins to recite the *fatiha*. I join them with my eyes open and make it through the first four lines.

"Aren't you fancy," Schwab says to me as he scratches the letters "USA" into the seat of the chair between his legs.

"Do you know the *fatiha*, *Jameela*?" Francis asks me.

"Hameed taught it to me," I say.

Francis puts back on his ball cap, which he removed for the *fatiha*, and begins to tell Schwab that his father was a sheik long ago, and Francis, before he began interpreting for the United States, was a special forces soldier under Saddam. Schwab nods periodically, either at Francis's story or at the progress of his artwork.

"My father was asked to administer a *fatiha* to one of the soldiers I fought with who died many years ago in Ramadi. My father had retired already, but was the best man for the job so he said, 'I will give the *fatiha*,' and drove to Ramadi and walked into the mosque, delivered the prayers. He said *Ameen* and then died of a heart attack. Yes, this is true," Francis says and sits back to shift his hat and mustache.

"At a proper *fatiha*," he says, "this is true, there will be coffee and someone reading the Quran."

I watch Schwab scratch a large penis into the armrest of his chair with his spring-assisted knife as a man walks around the circle with a Turkish coffee pot and two cups. Turkish coffee is thick, almost syrupy, and dark and nutty. You drink it black out of small cups and, unlike the chai, you don't add sugar. The coffee pots that serve Turkish coffee are gold or bronze. It looks like a genie might jump out of it instead of an opaque viscous liquid. The man comes to Francis and pours coffee into one of the cups.

"Ah," Francis says and nods. He takes the cup and sips.

The man pours Schwab a cup. Schwab swishes it around and sips.

Schwab and I hand our cups back to the man, who takes them, smiles at me, and continues down the line. Behind us, a recording of the Quran begins to play at an intolerable volume. Hameed continues his conversation with the man next to him, and Schwab resumes his artwork. Francis sits upright in his chair with his hands, palms down, on his knees and stares across the circle of chairs.

The recording abruptly stops when the coffee man has made the complete circle. Everyone stops talking and faces their palms up and begins the *fatiha* again. Men wipe their right hands over their faces, and Hameed and Francis get up to leave. Schwab and I follow them out.

"I THINK WE SHOULD JUST BLOW IT UP," TRAVIS SAYS. "JUST pack all this shit with C4 and call it good."

We are gathered around the operations center table again planning our exit. Perry tells me I am responsible for the disposition of all the property we will not drive out with us.

"Maybe we can just leave it here for the Iraqis," I say.

"Fuck that," Jordan says. "They'll sell it."

"Most of the stuff we're talking about is used beds and air conditioners and metal living containers with rusted-out roofs," I say.

"I bet we have enough C4. Or we could just set it on fire and call it good," Travis says.

"Jordan, I didn't sign up for a 1911," I say, noticing that someone has added my name to the list on the whiteboard behind Perry.

He looks away from his notepad, where he is sketching a cowboy having sex with a woman on top of a flaming mattress. "Yeah, but you wanted to, I can tell," he says.

"What about the terps?" Travis asks Perry. "Someone said they're about to let all the local nationals go."

"Do we have any local nationals?" Perry asks.

"I do," I say. Of the seven interpreters who work with my team, six are local nationals. Hameed is the only U.S. citizen, and the only one with a security clearance, which is why he was assigned to me. "When did this happen?" I ask.

"Yesterday," Travis says as he packs a wad of Grizzly into his lip and wipes his hands off on his pants. "Not sure when they have to be gone though."

"Is there anything we can do to prevent this from happening?" I ask Perry.

"You really do want a 1911," he says.

IT IS THE THIRD NIGHT OF THE *FATIHA*, THE NIGHT WHEN Francis tells me there will be a feast. I meet Hameed, Francis, and Schwab, who has decided to come for the feast, on the bench at 6:45 and head to the car. We drive to Hisham's building with the radio off.

"How could you not tell us it was going to happen?" Francis asks me.

"How could you not tell us it's going to happen?" Schwab asks.

"I didn't know," I say as we park and walk to rows of tables, where the chairs had been, behind Hisham's building.

Hisham greets us immediately, me first, then Hameed, then Schwab, then Francis, who says something extra to him. I watch as Hisham listens, then looks at me, and then shakes his head. "*La, la, la*," he says to Francis and leaves him to walk by my side. He brings us to a large table with huge bowls of rice prepared with fresh lamb and smaller bowls of roasted vegetables, *hubbuz*, and a bowl of sauce. Everyone there stands around and becomes silent. We face our palms up and recite the *fatiha*. I get through all seven verses but forget the *Ameen*. Hameed later tells me it took his wife three months to learn the complete *fatiha*, and she cried a lot.

Then we eat. There are no plates or utensils, so I watch for a bit while men gather rice into a piece of the bread, pack it with lamb, dip it into a sauce, and eat it with the same hands they wipe their faces with at the end of the prayer. I take a piece of bread, gather rice with it, place a piece of lamb inside, and dip it into the sauce bowl. One of the barbers (not Omar) smiles at me from across the table and passes me what looks like two jellyfish with no tentacles.

"What is that?" I ask Hameed, who stands to my right and eats.

"That's the roasted lamb fat. It's the best part," he says and reaches for it.

The barber looks at him and says, "*La, la, la,*" and points to me. I take one piece of cooked lamb fat, pack it into my piece of bread, and eat it. It is what I imagine eating a jellyfish feels like. I smile at the barber and say, "*Shukran, habibi.*" He blushes and leaves the table. I give the other to Schwab, who pokes it with his index finger and passes it to Hameed.

Hussein has come to mourn with Hisham. He finds me, stands close, and assembles bites of food for me. I smile at him as he passes me bread-wrapped lamb and waits as I dip it into the sauce. He smooths out his mustache with his left hand. Schwab laughs to himself next to me. All at once, the men step back from the table. Hisham's men come back and take the bowls of food away and replace them with dessert trays piled high with bananas, baklava, and what looks like a very tiny funnel cake made out of crystalized honey. Hussein picks up one of the tiny cakes and hands it to me and waits while I eat it. It is like eating granulated sugar and tastes waxy. While I eat this, Hussein peels a banana for me and hands it to me when I finish the cake. He smiles. Then he smooths his mustache.

Francis has been talking to Schwab for some time now, and Schwab shifts his weight back and forth between his feet as he eats baklavas. "My wife," Francis says, "once disagreed with me. This cannot happen. So I broke her arm. Yes, this is true," he says. "She did not do that again, and our son saw so now he understands too."

Schwab eats more baklava.

"We live here now. My wife, she works for Hussein. Her work is so good he gave us a car and a house with more than two rooms to live in. You see," he says, "she understands."

"What sort of work does your wife do for Hussein?" Schwab asks.

Francis takes a banana and walks away.

AT THE NIGHTLY OPERATIONS AND INTELLIGENCE MEET-
ing, we review targets. We get more information on high-ranking
members of particularly violent militias, and we discuss the missions they are planning to collect these targets for interrogation.
Guys express a need for more bullets and chem lights, yellow,
green, and infrared. They brief about the broken wide-capacity
map printer. They discuss which of the targets are being watched
by drones. Someone suggests we need to order more MREs.

"With the quantity someone already ordered," I say, "if we
line them up end to end, we will have 225 yards of MREs, which
means we will have to line about a third of the perimeter of this
compound seven feet deep with them. Hisham has also invited
us to eat at his dining hall."

Jordan makes an announcement for the 1911. "Last call," he
says. "Buy now and they'll be waiting for you when we get home."
My name is on the list.

When the meeting ends, I get up off the wooden bench to leave.
"Hey," Perry says.

"Yes, sir."

"Are you sure you don't want a 1911? It's a solid firearm. Smooth
action."

"I think I'm good, sir."

"You know," he says while he looks at a map of our compound,
"I was talking to Hussein. He told me about the guy who went tits
up. Then he asked me about tonight's mission. And I was thinking. Maybe the Iraqis got death right. We undersell it. But I bet
you it's a lot more peaceful than what we have going on here."

Ameen.

12

Pistol Whip

THE TEMPERATURES HAVE BEEN TOPPING 120 FOR DAYS now, and each time the heat rises to about 115 degrees, the generator turns off, cutting power to our entire compound. Our only recourse is to sit under the patio shaded with camouflage netting and wait for the generator to cool off enough to be restarted—a process that takes about four or five hours, depending on how much water we want to waste by emptying one-liter bottles over the generator and watching them instantly evaporate. I stay in the office as long as I can, telling Hameed that we will go meet with Adel, Hisham, and Ahmed once we lose power here. The Iraqis likely won't have power either. They are tapped into the Baghdad power supply, but when it is hot like this, their power rolls too, two or three hours on, two or three hours off, mitigated only by their sporadic willingness to turn on the backup generators.

Schwab sits in the chair on the opposite side of my desk, throwing magnetic darts at a Philadelphia Eagles dartboard left here by someone who affixed a Velcro patch with the name "Phillips" to the top. The magnets hardly ever hold, so Schwab throws the darts, watches them bounce off and land on top of the fridge or onto a computer, gathers them, and repeats the process. Last night our air force team in Basrah took heavy indirect fire overnight, and we haven't been able to get in contact with our guys down there. Schwab spoke briefly with the Navy Special Warfare Team in charge of the regional battalion, but they didn't know anything about our team. After Schwab told me about the attack, around 3:00 a.m., I called down to Kuwait to let our air force leadership know. No one answered, so I left a message.

While Schwab throws darts, I sit working at the classified computer on information cards for all the Iraqis I work with. Perry told me yesterday that it is suddenly vital to know the Iraqis' tribal affiliations, the strength of their allegiance to Saddam's regime, their religious sects, what we speculate they do on their leave periods, their other sources of income, our assessment of their marksmanship and, for some reason, the length and pattern of their facial hair. As I speculate what Hazbar does on his leave period—tends his date palm farm in Diyala, harvests watermelons and peaches he brings back for me, plays with his five-year-old son, Ali, kisses his wife—the phone rings.

"Schifani," I say when I pick up. Perry instructed me to never answer the phone with my rank or my unit. We assume everyone in Iraq can hear us.

"Is this Captain Katherine Schifani, from SOITT?" says the voice. My air force chain of command, headquartered some four hundred miles south of here in Kuwait, insists on using rank and unit over the phone. Fortunately, they never actually know what unit we are a part of. For the last three rotations, we were SOITT, though people forget what all the letters mean. In March, when the army reorganized us, we were parceled out to six different units, all with new acronyms that we don't know all the letters to either. After three months of trying to explain our new, fractured organization to my air force leadership, I stopped trying to accurately express our status. Part of the issue is that we haven't had reliable email communication with Kuwait since the reorg, as I had noted every Tuesday by conference call when I delivered our personnel status. I recently stopped joining the conference call, just to see if anyone would notice. It has been two months and so far no one has commented on it, meaning no one has received our personnel status for two months either, except through phone messages announcing the unknown status of two of our team members in Basrah.

"Yes," I say.

"Good," says the voice. "This is Major Jones, your operations officer down here with the 467th."

"Okay," I say.

"Did you get the email I sent you? You haven't responded," he says.

"No, sir," I say.

"Right," Major Jones says. On the phone, he sounds like the kind of man who wears Brut cologne, even on the border of a war zone, keeps his hair extremely and evenly short, tries to grow a mustache on leave knowing that it only grows in patches, and took two tries to qualify on his pistol.

He forgets he has met me. He was responsible for greeting us when we landed in Kuwait in February after forty-four hours of continuous travel that started on a bus in New Jersey. After we were in-processed; issued body armor, helmets, and first aid kits; and ushered to temporary lodging tents and trailers, he walked Schwab to the coffee shop on base to discuss all our important information over vanilla frappe coffee. After he paid for Schwab's coffee, Schwab told him I was the one in charge. Major Jones left Schwab at the coffee shop, put all the papers in a blue folder, handed it to me, and walked back to his office to finish his frappe and prepare for the official squadron briefing, which he delivered more or less accurately.

Slide 1: A map showing Iraq and Kuwait. He told us the squadron fought hard to maintain a command presence in Iraq, but that they were now based in Kuwait to support the drawdown.

Slide 2: A map of Iraq and lots of dark blue squiggly lines. He told us they fly some sixty thousand miles on helicopters to come see all of us. He looked at Schwab and nodded.

Slide 3: An air force guy with a badly formed mustache wearing dark sunglasses and holding a long rifle with no magazine loaded. He told us we were the heartbeat of the army's operations in Iraq; he told us that our squadron motto is "Pound for pound, we do more" because we so vastly outperform our army counterparts in the same job.

Slides 4 and 5: Self-portraits of Major Jones in body armor, smiling, recognizably at a base even farther from Iraq than this one. He told us about his last deployment.

Slides 6–10: Pictures of his wife featuring all three colors of her hair. He smiled around the room, skipping me and the rest of the women on my team.

Slides 11–13: Pictures of Major Jones and his wife on a beach somewhere tropical, holding drinks with miniature umbrellas, one photo of them near a waterslide. He reminded us he was away from his family as well, and he looked at Schwab and nodded.

Slide 14: Our chain of command, featuring official pictures of our squadron commander—who could not give the briefing herself because she worked day shift, which didn't start for an hour—of Major Jones, and of someone else he didn't introduce. He told us that if we suddenly were not being used within our job specialty, we should tell them right away and they would talk to the army and move us to jobs within our specialty or send us home.

And here we are, filling out special forces profile cards and waiting to hear if a supply troop and a vehicle mechanic who are in Basrah augmenting Navy SEALs are still alive.

And I am on the phone with Major Jones. "We need your whole team to complete the Don't Ask Don't Tell repeal training online ASAP. We need the whole squadron done by tonight."

"Okay," I say. "We will not likely have it done tonight."

"What's the problem?" he asks.

"I probably won't be able to get a hold of everyone on my team by tonight, and our guys at the outstations don't have internet that can access the training website. Actually, neither do we," I tell him.

"So you can have it done by Friday?" he asks.

"Yes, sir," I say. At least by Friday we can figure out how to fabricate the certificate you print off after completing computer-based training modules like this.

"Good," he says. "Send me an email when you're 100 percent compliant."

"We don't have email that can send to your accounts," I say.

"Look forward to hearing from you by Friday, Captain. Pound for pound . . . ," he says and pauses.

"I said pound for pound, Captain," the major repeats.

"Schifani copies. Out," I say. When I talk to the men I work with, which rarely happens over the phone, we speak like we are on radios. We also assume that the reason for phone calls is only to pass important information. I hang up the phone. Schwab collects the darts and begins to throw them again.

"What was that about?" he asks.

"Some computer-based training that Kuwait wants us to do," I say.

He throws a dart at the Phillips Velcro patch. The phone rings again.

"Schifani," I say.

"Captain Schifani, of SOITT?" says the same voice, emitting Brut through the receiver.

"Yes," I say, and I put the phone on speaker for Schwab.

"Major Jones again, from the 467th down here in Kuwait."

"Yes, sir."

"You're actually overdue on that CBT. We need it done before lunch today so we can report this up to Ninth Air Expeditionary Task Force. Can you do that?"

"No, sir."

"Look, I know you have other things you need to work on, but this is the general's hottest item right now. We're the only unit in the command who is still noncompliant. I recommend getting your team together in a room and just going through the slides together. Then you can knock the whole thing out in less than an hour."

"Okay, sir. I won't be able to talk to my whole team. I can meet with six of them in an hour or so, but our internet doesn't get the CBT here."

"Okay, then you need to find an MWR tent and do it in there," he says.

"We don't have an MWR tent," I say. We used to, but the unit Schwab works for took over management of our compound after the reorg and turned the plywood MWR building into their operations center and locked the doors with keypads they won't give us the codes to. They store a lot of gear in there, have taken all the internet jacks, and hide boxes of desirable cereal in the back.

"Look, Captain, I don't know what kind of conditions you have out there, but you need to get this done and call me back as soon as you're finished."

"Okay, sir, we're finished," Schwab says as he leans over the desk to join the conversation, holding a handful of featherless metal darts.

"How is that possible?" the major asks.

"We've done as much as we can," Schwab says. This is why Schwab has such a tenuous relationship with his unit here, why they only help him when not doing so has a direct and devastating effect on their own operations, why they won't give us the codes and why they take our Lucky Charms, and why, by extension, they hate all of us. This is also why Schwab is so useful.

"Captain," says the major, apparently unable to distinguish my voice from Schwab's, "this isn't a joking matter. The general is tracking how many of his troops haven't done the CBT. Your team is the only one that hasn't even started. We've been sending emails for two weeks now. We're getting chewed out in our staff meetings because we're still in the red. You need to do the training and call me back ASAP when it's done."

"Yes, sir," I say. Schwab throws the darts all at once; one actually stays affixed to the dartboard.

I hang up the phone and watch as Schwab gets out of the chair to collect the darts. "Any word from Basrah?" I ask him, as though he may have heard something while sitting in my office throwing metal spears at the wall. He looks at me with an open mouth and shakes his head. "Close the door," I tell him.

He sets the quiver down on my desk next to the stapler, gets up, closes the door, and secures it shut with a piece of bailing wire and a protruding screw.

Schwab and Shawn, a staff sergeant we sent to Diyala, are the only people on my team younger than I am, and Schwab only by a month. He's also the only other officer here and by default the only air force person I can talk to. I had no plans of telling anyone here anything about my life, other than I hate Shreveport and I like the snow. I imagine myself like Tom Hanks's character in *Saving Private Ryan*, distant, enigmatic, commanding. But Tom Hanks's character in the movie never got phone calls about completing a CBT from a man who spent more time showing us pictures of his wife in a bikini than he did explaining what to do if we needed help. As I break down in front of Schwab, crying big, angry tears and shaking with rage, he grabs the darts, moves his chair back a little from the desk, and smirks to himself because he knows this place has finally cracked me, at least for a few minutes, and he's been waiting for this.

From the U.S. Air Force Don't Ask Don't Tell Repeal Training, Tier 3, a narrated twenty-four-slide presentation

Slide 3: What's new?

>No discharge based on sexual orientation

>Not a factor in recruitment and retention

What has NOT changed?

>Evaluation based on merit, fitness and capability

>Sexual misconduct = grounds for administrative or legal action

Slide 8: What if . . .

>I have moral or religious concerns?

>>Rights

>>>Free exercise of religious expression, within law and policy, remains unchanged

        Maintain beliefs

        Discuss concerns with commander/chaplain

    Responsibilities

        Continue to treat all with dignity and respect

        Continue to follow all lawful orders

Slide 10: What if . . .

    I want an early discharge

        No policy for early discharge based on:

        Opposition to repeal

        Opposition to serving or living with gay, lesbian or bisexual members

        Provision for voluntary discharge remains the same, and is granted only when in the best interest of the Air Force

Slide 13: How does this policy affect . . .

    Equal treatment?

        All Airmen shall be evaluated only on individual merit, fitness and capability

        Use of existing mechanisms such as chain of command, IG, etc., for redress of issues based on sexual orientation

Slide 24: Summary

    Brief Provided:

        Information regarding DADT and its effects

        Reminders of:

        Air Force Core Values

        Air Force diversity and unit cohesion

        Standards of conduct

        Until the date of repeal, current policy remains in effect

The day Schwab sat smirking in my office with a handful of magnetic darts and found out that I have a girlfriend, our relationship dramatically improved. He now takes notes at meetings I run, he asks my opinion on tasks that, ultimately, I am responsible for anyway, and he walks into my office in the morning and shows me naughty messages he sends to his wife, who is currently in Afghanistan. On particularly hot mornings, he comes in and shows me lewd internet memes. The one he shows me this morning is of a man performing oral sex on his female partner with the caption "Breakfast is the most important meal." Schwab pulls up the picture on my unclassified computer (which can't access official air force sites but can access this), steps back from my desk, adjusts the belt holding his pistol, and laughs.

He sits down in the chair and grabs the darts. "Are you into strap-ons?" he asks.

"What?"

"Probably not," he says and squints at me. "You look like more of a purist." He taps the computer monitor with one of the darts and winks. He is leaving this evening for Diyala to check on our guys out there. One of them has had a stun grenade thrown into his room twice in the last three weeks. The team leader out there told me they did it so he would learn to lock his door. Now that he locks his door, they have taken the steps away from the doorway so he will make an unexpected three-foot drop in the morning. I ask the team leader to stop harassing my supply troop, but the supply troop rarely works and is rarely effective when he does. Unlike the other member of our team in Diyala, who is generally proactive and communicates frequently with us, our supply troop forgot to call in for accountability (again) on Monday and lost another supply request for the team, so Schwab is going out to serve him paperwork.

Schwab walks around my desk and grabs the darts. I would be going with him to Diyala except that Perry has assigned me an urgent task here. I am to find out an accurate count of the ammunition the Iraqi brigade—including all three battalions and the support unit—has by type and quantity. I need this by 7:00 p.m. tomorrow. I know that Ahmed has this information somewhere. But in all my months here, he has yet to disclose the brigade totals. I know the First Battalion's totals because Mara shares those with me any time I ask, but the commander of the Second Battalion won't talk to me. Hisham has no ammunition. Adel photocopied his totals and gave them to me in a neatly organized folder when I asked. The brigade, he told me, has an additional store that Ahmed alone has the keys to.

"I have to go see Ahmed," I tell Schwab as I close the computer and collect my notebook.

"You should show him that picture," Schwab says.

Schwab has never worked with Ahmed. He doesn't understand why I did not want a smaller-sized uniform that fits better when offered. He doesn't understand why I haven't bothered to fix the unfortunate, now months-old, haircut a former Iraqi commando gave me. He does not understand why I choose to brandish my pistol instead of conceal it like the rest of the men here. He does not understand why I got rid of the shackles left for me in the bottom desk drawer in this office.

Like many Iraqis that I work with, Ahmed has a dark, full mustache that bends slightly down the sides of his mouth—something I note on my info card. He offers me cigarettes every time I go to see him, and when I decline, he requests that I draw one out of the pack for him. I have managed to refuse this task for months by pretending that I don't understand what he is asking me to do, keeping my hand over my heart, and shaking my head. Instead, Ahmed waits uncomfortably long and then walks over to the woman with electric-blue eye makeup, who slowly removes cigarettes from Ahmed's pack and places them in his mouth. He does not let her light them.

By now, I know that when Ahmed is on leave, she is not here. The Iraqi sergeant major that works here tells me stories about them. Ahmed is married and has a few kids in North Baghdad. But when he is at work and on post, he lives with the woman in the office. Her entire family, the sergeant major tells me, was killed by Saddam's men, right before the U.S. invasion, over a misunderstanding about what they intended to do with a field they purchased outside of Ramadi. The woman found their bodies in sections strewn across the field one afternoon, and in the near darkness that night she fled Ramadi to Baghdad. Somehow, in the course of the next four years, she ended up here, where she has been for half a decade, living with Ahmed, slowly drawing his cigarettes.

She never speaks to me. Sometimes she nods when Ahmed speaks, but she cannot maintain eye contact with me for more than a moment. Today, when Hameed and I arrive at the office, she is the first one I see.

"*Assalam alaykum*," I say to her and extend my hand like I do with the men.

"*Wa alaykumas salam*," she says, puts her limp hand in mine, looks at my boots, lets go, and leaves the office.

Ahmed and the sergeant major are the only ones here. I greet both of them, and Ahmed offers me a cigarette.

"*La, la, saydie, shukran*," I say and hold my hand over my heart.

He holds the box and waves it around in front of me. I shake my head. He looks for the woman, who has not returned, before he puts the pack back on his desk and leans back in his chair.

"*Chaku maku, Jameela?*" he asks me. What's new?

"*Maku chi, maku chi*," I say. Not much.

He calls for chai, explains something about the computer not working, and rearranges blank folders on his desk. The chai arrives and, as we sip, the power cuts off. Ahmed gets up, opens the window behind him, and lets in the Iraqi summer and light. The window is the only one in this room and is covered with an elaborate pattern of woven iron and translucent yellow contact paper. When closed, it is almost entirely opaque. With the window open behind him, Ahmed sits back down in his leather chair and glows. The heat feels like it is radiating off his uniform. The sergeant major hits the computer and gets up. He shakes my hand on the way out and smiles. Ahmed interlocks his hands behind his head and looks at me. He can sense I need something from him and relishes the power.

"*Saydie*," I say, "I need to know the total number of rounds by type in the brigade. I don't know Second Battalion's totals, and I don't know how much is in the brigade reserve."

Hameed interprets. Ahmed frowns at the part I imagine to be the brigade reserve. He wonders how I know and which of his countrymen betrayed his trust by telling me.

"One million rounds of each," he says and Hameed interprets.

"How do you know?" I ask.

He sits back up in his chair and opens a blank folder. "One million of each except smoke grenades, only thirty-two of those," he says. Hameed interprets.

I open my notebook and angle it to the light of the window behind him. On a table I made with a ruler and semi-functional government-issued blue pen, I have a column for each type of ammunition and the totals so far (from First and Third Battalions). I make sure he can see the table as I read off some of the amounts I have.

"500,000 rounds loose 7.62; 247,000 rounds 7.62 link; 123,200 rounds .50 cal."

He nods as I read. I look up.

"Why do you need to know?" he asks me and Hameed interprets.

"We are trying to establish a process that will resupply you long-term. In order to do that, we need to know how much you have so we can order more."

"Who will pay?"

"For now," I say, "we will." He doesn't know that this is only sort of true. Mostly Perry wants to know how many rounds the Iraqis have in case things turn against us here after the withdrawal and we have to hold them off at the walls to our compound. He and his guys are trying to figure out how long we could last.

Ahmed smiles. He will do anything if it means that he will get more American goods. As the brigade director of logistics, he and the Iraqi general he works for equate his value to the number of things he counts and controls.

"We are particularly interested in the amount of 9mm pistol rounds you have," I say. Ahmed is the only non-commando here who wears a pistol. The grip of his pistol is gold plated, but to assure me it still fires, and that he can fire it, he once took me out to the trash pile and shot birds with it until he was satisfied—also information I have noted in my card on him.

He smiles again. "Come back at 2300," he says and Hameed interprets. "Don't be late."

Hameed and I drive back to our compound, where I pick up Schwab and his battle buddy and drive them to the landing zone to wait for their ride.

AT QUARTER OF ELEVEN, I MEET HAMEED BY THE CAMOUFLAGE-net canopy, and we leave to go see Ahmed. We park outside the brigade headquarters building that houses his office and walk into the blue-tinted light of the entryway. Their groundskeeper is a silhouette in the darkness watering the plants and cleaning dust off the sidewalk. Music plays through speakers hidden in shrubs behind him. We wave and go inside. Ahmed is in his office with the woman, who slowly draws a cigarette for him, places it in his mouth, and leaves the room, looking at the floor, without saying hello. Ahmed lights his cigarette and motions us to sit down. He swivels around in his chair to open the window for ventilation. He looks at his watch and says something to Hameed, which Hameed doesn't interpret. Then he looks at me. "*Chaku maku?*" he says.

"*Maku chi, saydie. Maku chi.*"

He offers me a cigarette and smiles when I decline. He opens the top drawer of his dark-cherry desk and takes out a folder. Inside the folder is a stack of stapled yellow paper stamped at the bottom with the brigade seal. He puts out his cigarette, closes the window, and hands me the yellow piece of paper with English numbers and Arabic explanations of the types of ammunition. Hameed and I stand up, and I watch as he begins to translate them. 5.56 ball, 5.56 trace, 7.62 loose, 7.62 link, .50 cal, det cord, grenades, incendiary grenades, smoke grenades (green, yellow, purple), C4. The 9mm ammunition has its own page. Ahmed walks around the table, stands directly in front of me, takes off his pistol, drops the magazine, picks up a pen, and adds fifteen more rounds of 9mm to the list.

"*Khamsa'tash*," he says. The power cuts out.

I can hear Hameed sit down in the complete darkness behind me and begin to fish for his cell phone to use as a flashlight. I smell Ahmed's cigarette-flavored breath suddenly inches from my face. I hear him reload the magazine.

"*Ah, Jameela*," he says in a low, drawn-out whisper.

I feel him put the grip of his pistol sideways against my chest; the back of his hand rubs a figure eight over my breasts. He inhales. As he exhales, he presses his hand across my chest and moves the pistol so it points directly through me. He drags it down to my left hip, opposite my own weapon, and points behind me at Hameed, who is discovering he does not have his cell phone with him tonight. I know the hammer is forward. I can feel his thumb on the inside of my right thigh as he moves the pistol down between my legs, pointed at the ground, and I wonder if there is a round in the chamber, if it really should be sixteen more. He pushes the top of the receiver hard against me and drags it the length of the pistol, from the front sight to the rear sight, until the rear sight snags on the bottom of my zipper. He breathes Marlboro on me and moves the pistol back toward him again until the front sight catches my pant seam. He audibly inhales, and he moves the pistol forward again. Each time he covers me with stale tobacco breaths, he works the pistol between my legs. He breathes in as he pulls it back toward him and exhales when he pushes it away. His hand starts to tremble around the gold-plated grip. He pushes harder.

I think I should shoot him. But my arms stay where they are, frozen in place by the stale, blank 90-degree air of this concrete Iraqi building, my left hand holding the paper on his desk with a total that increased by fifteen rounds moments ago, my right hand resting on my own pistol, still secured in its holster, aimed at the floor. Outside, I hear the backup generator kick on. The smell of his cigarette breath gets weaker, and he steps back from me as the lights come back on. He reholsters his pistol and smiles at me. While the lights were out, the woman with the blue eye makeup returned in total darkness and sat down at a desk behind Ahmed. "*Naqeeb Jameela*," Ahmed says as he walks around his desk and sits down. The woman stares at me deeply, her blue-framed eyes holding mine. We can't look away. I hear Hameed say something to Ahmed behind me.

"He wants to know if you need anything else," Hameed says to me.

"No," I say, take the papers, and walk out without shaking hands with Ahmed. The woman stands up and says, "*Ma'asalaama*."

Hameed and I get in the car. He finds his cell phone sitting on the seat. "He was in a weird mood," he says.

"We got the numbers," I say and start the car. We drive back to our compound, where I let Hameed out and take the list to Perry.

"Here you go," I say to him and hand it over.

"What is this?" he asks me.

"The brigade ammunition totals you asked for."

"Oh. Well, we ended up just making something up. We probably can't trust their count anyhow."

"So you don't need this?"

"Not really. But I'm impressed you could get it. Brandon has been trying for months, and he hasn't gotten anywhere. What did you have to do to get them?"

13

Design Flaws

IT WAS A BAD DESIGN FROM THE BEGINNING, EIGHT YEARS in the making. As I stand here and look at it, I can see it has only gotten worse. For starters, the door isn't big enough to get the forklift through, which is an even bigger problem because the forklift is already inside and there is not yet a floor. This warehouse was supposed to house spare gun and vehicle parts, but so far, three years into its construction, all that's here is a two-story mess of scaffolding—supporting much of the weight of the clay and bricks—and dark, square rooms. It looks less like a warehouse than the type of motel you might find under an overpass with peeling stucco and door frames in mismatched colors. The fact that there is only one way to the second floor (an unlit set of stairs that occupies an entire room in the corner) reinforces the creepy feeling.

The warehouse's only inhabitants are the three men responsible for its construction. Two of these men are named Ali, and the other man's name I have never heard spoken. The two Alis are builders; the nameless man cooks them food using a propane burner and trash-can lids. I get out of my car and watch as he stirs a red rice mixture on one of the lids and smokes a cigarette outside the motel. He takes the cigarette out of his mouth and waves at me as I walk toward the too-narrow-for-a-forklift door with my substitute interpreter.

Sometimes Hameed is just "away" and no one knows, or will tell me, where, but he shows up when we get ready to drive to the air base for dinner. In Hameed's absence, I take Cain with me to the warehouse-motel for the monthly inspection I was told I am supposed to conduct. Cain is a local national interpreter from Baghdad whose parents disowned him once he decided to help the Americans. He is only a few months away from his American visa and hopes that the three years he has been working with us will help the process along.

All our local national interpreters chose their English names early on in the war, because they figured the Americans would never learn or pronounce their Arabic names. Cain has never told us why he chose his name, and he is the only one of the local nationals who has told us his Arabic name (Saif), which a few of us have started using. We don't quite get the inflection, but he is okay with us calling him Safe and smiles when we try to say it correctly. He is tall and skinny and dresses in mostly black with a studded black leather belt and a lot of cologne. I once overheard him tell the guy he regularly interprets for that he thinks when he gets to America his acne will go away the second he steps off the airplane. He wears a lot of gel in his hair, which slowly melts when he is outside for too long.

When the cook sees Cain, he stops waving and starts yelling at him. Cain walks over to the man to shake hands, but the cook yells at him and throws his hands up over his head and walks away to tend the rice.

"What was that about?" I ask him.

"It was nothing," he says. "He wanted to offer you lunch, but he didn't know I was coming and I cannot eat their food."

"Why not?"

"Because I'm from Baghdad and now live here," he says.

"Aren't they also from Baghdad and now live here?"

"Yes," he says and ducks scaffolding to walk through the front door.

When we get inside, the builders are sitting in the shade of the forklift drawing in the dirt. I greet them and they stand up to shake my hand. Both of them look at Cain and nod, but they don't shake hands with him.

I ask them what progress they have made since last month, and Cain interprets. They point to the staircase in the corner, where they converted the lower half of the stairs to concrete instead of mud like the top half. They have done this by pouring concrete directly over the mud, apparently without leveling or flattening the stairs first. Cain asks them another question and they both shrug.

"They say they have no money to do the rest," Cain says.

One of the men nods, points to where they cook, on the outside of the wall, and says something else.

"They only have food because they are cousins of one of the generals here, and he has been bringing them rice and bread," Cain interprets. "But they have no money to finish the warehouse or to eat without that."

I shade my face from the sun, now directly overhead and shining down through the gap in the center where there is not yet a roof, and look at the warehouse. According to some papers I found in the middle desk drawer—under a smoke grenade, a box of neon-green sticky notes, and a set of handcuffs—when I first arrived, the United States has funded this warehouse project from the beginning, so far paying almost one and a half million dollars for an unroofed, unfloored motel with sixteen square rooms, no electricity, a door too narrow for the forklift already inside, and a second story too tall for the trapped forklift to reach. I can see where the builders have laid their bedrolls on the floor of one of the rooms that doesn't get much sun through the open roof.

"They said you need to get them more money," Cain says. "You don't do that anymore, do you?" he asks me.

"I don't know," I say and climb onto the left fork of the forklift to try to look at the second floor, supported on two sides entirely by steel tube scaffolding.

"DO YOU THINK THEY'LL CELEBRATE?" MILLER ASKS NO one in particular. He sits on the horseshoe bench with Sarah, the plumber; Jeremy, a vehicle mechanic, who has a very narrow mustache that doesn't go all the way to the end of his mouth and was at an outstation for a few months before coming back here; Schwab; and me.

"Who?" Sarah asks him.

"The gays," he says. The official repeal is a few weeks away.

"I think they'll be happy they won't be fired for nothing," Sarah says.

Schwab looks at me.

"I'm tired," I say and get up and go back to my room to consider running.

Perry finds me running on the treadmill facing the wall of the tan tent with only three working overhead lights, which all emit a strange blue glow. He taps his finger on the side of the treadmill and waits for me to take my headphones off.

"You need to come with me to the funding meeting," he says. "They have some questions about the first aid kits you want to order."

"When is the meeting?" I ask him without slowing down.

"One hour," he says. "Up the street."

When he says "up the street," he means out two gates, down the road for twenty or thirty minutes, and in two more gates, through another gate, which is actually secure, and into a building with no windows. In that building is the teleconference room, with a giant screen and solid dark-oak table. Pictures of all the Green Berets who have died in this country since the start of the war flank the walls of the room.

I drop the speed of the treadmill to a fast walk and try to remember that I was three and a half miles short for today's run.

A FEW DAYS AGO, A COLONEL WHO I DON'T ACTUALLY WORK for sent me an email saying I had two weeks to spend $49 million for the Iraqis. When I tried to call him and ask what I could possibly spend $49 million on in two weeks, his interpreter informed me he was on leave and would return to the country in about three weeks. I asked Perry, who I do sort of work for, what I could spend

$49 million on in two weeks, and he suggested more guns. After a few more phone calls to people I've never met, a few lawyers, a few people from the security cooperation office in the Green Zone, and one guy from Alabama, I learned it takes quite a lot of paperwork and congressional approval to buy $49 million worth of guns. So instead, I put together a package to spend the money on first aid kits, beds, air conditioners, a backhoe, an industrial grader, a fire truck, basic hospital sterilization equipment, a surgical cauterizer, and a dump truck for the Iraqis. All told, I was only able to request about $13 million worth of air conditioners, first aid kits, bed frames, and hospital equipment.

THE TELECONFERENCE VIDEO FEED IS BROKEN. INSTEAD of the panel of people known simply as "The Council of Colonels" appearing as a panel of people, they show up on the screen as some kind of Jackson Pollock knock-off, with strange magenta streaks disrupting an otherwise desert-green and tan color scheme positioned in front of what might be the U.S. flag and the army flag. This council decides how money gets spent on this country. I was last here requesting better armor for the Iraqi vehicle fleet, a $1.5-million modification to a contract that had been paid in full but so far had produced only two of the sixty vehicles promised. Instead of adding more armor, the council increased the number of vehicles and declared that they can just use a new one when their old ones break. Bombs, I tried to explain, were the issue, not breakdowns.

"Isn't that the same thing, Captain?" one of the colonels asked me and denied my $1.5 million modification but approved the $6 million increase in the fleet size.

Today, I have a stack of papers in front of me that detail why the Iraqis need the first aid kits and the rest of the items I requested. Perry glances over at my notes and points at one line I have written by both the hospital equipment and the first aid kits.

"You can't say that," he says.

I cross out *Because Abu Rahim bled out on that roof in Khaz-*

amiya and shouldn't have. The audio feed flicks on, and the council members begin to introduce themselves. Four other locations that have funding requests announce their attendance; then Perry introduces us as the representatives from our unit.

We are first on the agenda. I begin to explain why the items on the list are essential to continued operations in our area when one of the magenta streaks unmutes himself on the other end and interrupts me.

"Captain, are you a mathematician?"

"No, sir," I answer.

"You have here that you want to buy all three thousand of your Iraqis a first aid kit, is that right?"

"Yes, sir. One thousand for the commandos here, one thousand for the regional battalions, and one thousand spares. Three thousand total."

"But your total price for these is $450,000."

"Yes, sir, they are $150 each," I say as the screen begins to move side to side like a bad optical illusion.

"Do the math, Captain. For $450,000 at $150 a pop you're going to buy three hundred thousand first aid kits. That's enough for the whole damn Iraqi army for the next fifteen years."

Another colonel in the Magic Eye laughs, and the first magenta streak motions for a vote. They deny the funding request by a vote of 5–0 before I have a chance to offer a different view of division.

The Council of Colonels reviews our requests in order. They approve the hospital equipment because one of them thinks that we might also use the hospital, and therefore it should have sterilization equipment, even though the items we buy here today won't actually reach this country for another year or two. They deny the beds and air conditioners, approve the dump truck, and deny the rest. Then the first magenta streak asks about the warehouse.

"Says here that you need another $2 million for the brigade warehouse project."

Perry, who up until now has been cleaning his fingernails with a spring-assisted knife, unmutes our end of the audio feed and looks at me.

"Actually, sir, I think it is best if we abandon that project. The builders have not made any significant progress in the last seven months, and it does not appear that they have appropriately handled the original money we allocated for the facility."

"So give up?" he asks.

"Perhaps," I say, "we could simply redirect that money to a project with more immediate needs and better spending oversight."

The council votes 4–1 to approve another $2 million for the warehouse and moves on to the next location on their agenda.

The group from Basrah requests money to install three 47-inch flat-screen TVs in their operations center. When the council reminds the Basrah group that the money has to be spent on the Iraqis, the person tells them that Iraqis often enter their facility. Approved 3–2.

Next the Basrah group requests $50,000 in cash to pay some Iraqis who open and close a gate on Tuesday. Approved 5–0.

While the group from Mosul attempts to justify their funding needs, Perry slips me a piece of paper that says: *All LN terps have to be gone by tomorrow night—no $ left for them.*

I look at him and mute the audio.

"Do they know?" I ask him.

"I found out an hour ago. So probably."

WE PULL BACK INTO OUR COMPOUND, AND PERRY LETS ME off near the trailer where I work before he goes back to his side. I walk inside to put my papers down and find Beck sitting at his desk flipping through the first few pages of a small camouflaged copy of the Psalms and New Testament.

"They released all the LNs," he says to me.

"I know, I heard."

"All of them. By tomorrow."

I nod and sit down.

"Do you have the phone number for a chaplain?" he asks me.

"What happened?"

He closes the book and tells me that he started telling the LNs. Brad has family up north and is going to go back to being a chemical engineer with his wife. Francis and his wife have a house on base, because Francis's wife works for Hussein. David found a transfer to another unit in Karbala. Saif found out and began to cry.

"He can't go home," Beck says.

"I know."

"What about his visa?"

Jeremy, Saif's regular U.S. adviser for the last few months, opens the door. Panting, he says, "He's in Sarah's room. With a gun. Pointed at himself."

We get up and run to Sarah's room. Saif had been teaching Sarah Arabic every afternoon for a few months. We find her sitting outside her window in tears speaking through the screen.

"He won't listen," she says to me. "Tell him it's okay. It's okay." She says something in Arabic through the screen, and Saif yells back in English, "They're going to kill me. I should save them the trouble."

Beck opens the door and we walk in. Saif sits on Sarah's bed, leaning up against the thin divider wall that separates her room from the one next door. When we come through the door, he turns the gun toward us. Beck reaches for his holster and I grab his hand.

"Saif, please," I say to him.

He looks at the pistol, turning it toward himself, and looks down the barrel. He raises his left hand so it's even with his right, still holding the pistol, and examines the backs of his hands. He turns his left hand over and looks at the palm. "My hands!" he yells and drops the gun to look at both palms, and he starts to weep.

Outside, Sarah, still crying, comes in and sits on the floor.

Beck walks over to him and takes the gun away. Its safety is off and the hammer is back, but there is no magazine. Beck taps me on the shoulder, and we walk outside while Sarah and Jeremy weep with Saif.

"WE CAN'T KEEP HIM HERE," BECK SAYS. "WE CAN'T PAY him."

"But he could stay just for a little, until he knows what he can do," Jeremy says.

"Whose pistol was that?" I ask.

"I can bring him food back every time I go," Jeremy says.

"They won't send a chaplain for a non-U.S. person," Beck says. "And he could have shot me."

"He didn't," Jeremy says to him. "What about his visa? He's almost one of us."

"Almost," Beck says.

SARAH DROPPED SAIF OFF AT THE OUTSIDE GATE OF THE largest U.S. compound in Iraq on a Tuesday afternoon in late August. He had one bag with all his black clothes and hair gel and cologne. He was the last of our LNs to leave. Now that they are gone, we have to take turns working. Since he is from Bakersfield, California, Hameed is our only interpreter left. Beck and I sit in the trailer and wait for him to come back from the power plant, where he and Sarah are helping troubleshoot a faulty generator.

"Was that right, making him leave?" I ask Beck.

"He couldn't stay here. It wasn't safe. For any of us, but especially not for Jeremy or Sarah."

"It's not safe for him anywhere."

Beck shrugs and asks how the funding meeting went.

HAMEED AND I ARE ON THE WAY BACK TO THE WAREHOUSE to tell them more funding was approved. When we arrive, all three men are outside under the scaffolding, leaning against the wall. Their bedrolls are also outside under the scaffolding. They stand up when they see the car and walk over to greet us. We shake hands and one of them looks at Hameed and says, "We are done building."

"It's not done," I say. "In fact, your funding just got approved and you'll have enough to finish the floors and roof."

"*La, la, la,*" they say.

"No?" I ask. "Why not?"

"Design flaws," Hameed interprets.

Then Hameed begins to talk to them. They point to the base's perimeter wall, just a few dozen feet from the west wall of the warehouse, and make arching motions with their hands. One of them opens his eyes wide and grabs onto the other one, while sweeping his hand in front of him like he's moving a shower curtain out of the way. The builder he's holding raises his hands and grabs one of them at the wrist with his other hand. The cook points at the second story and takes a step back.

Hameed nods until they stop talking.

"Someone broke in last night," he says.

"How do you break into a place that has no door?" I ask.

"They left something."

"Left what?" I ask.

"These men didn't look, not really, but they can't work anymore in there."

I walk past the men through the door and wait for Hameed. He shakes his head at me and doesn't move. The men take a step back from the wall. Inside, in the center of the dirt floor, is a human hand, severed at the wrist. It didn't bleed much where it is; it just sits there in the dirt, palm toward the sky. I stare at the hand without getting any closer to it. I can hear Hameed and the men talking behind me on the other side of the open door.

I look up through the roofless structure at the sun. It's almost noon, and directly overhead. When I look back down, I notice something in one of the second-story rooms. I shade my eyes with my left hand and see what looks like a shoe, attached to what might be a black pant leg hanging off the ledge of one of the corner rooms. It's still dark enough I can't really see it, especially not after looking at the sun, but in the same corner as the shoe on the ground floor is the other hand, in the shade, palm up to the sky. I step back toward the door, looking at the hands, at the shoe, at the sun.

"They moved just the one in the middle," Hameed says to me as I come out. "To see if it was real."

One of the builders hands me a half-empty bottle of water and I drink it.

"I think I did this," I say to Hameed.

"What?"

"Don't tell them, Hameed." I look at the men, who are waiting for Hameed to interpret my words.

"What should I say?" he asks. "Can you fix this?"

Insha'allah.

Source Acknowledgments

Earlier versions of some chapters previously appeared in the following publications:

"Cartography": *Epiphany*, 2015 Chapbook Contest
"*Elhamdullah*": *Consequence*, January 2, 2018
"The Kill List": *Southeast Review* 33, no. 1
"The Omars": *Consequence* 7 (Spring 2015)
"Pistol Whip": *Iowa Review* 45, no. 1 (Spring 2015)